SRA ART Connections

Level 1

Authors

Rosalind Ragans, Ph.D., Senior Author

Willis "Bing" Davis   Jane Rhoades Hudak, Ph.D.   Bunyan Morris
Tina Farrell   Gloria McCoy   Nan Yoshida

Contributing Author

Jackie Ellett

Education Division
The Music Center of Los Angeles County

Columbus, OH

The McGraw-Hill Companies

Authors

Senior Author
Dr. Rosalind Ragans, Ph.D.
Associate Professor Emerita
Georgia Southern University

Willis "Bing" Davis
Associate Professor Emeritus
Central State University - Ohio
President & Founder of
SHANGO: The Center for the
Study of African American
Art & Culture

Tina Farrell
Assistant Superintendent
Curriculum and Instruction
Clear Creek Independent
School District,
League City, Texas

Jane Rhoades Hudak, Ph.D.
Professor of Art
Georgia Southern University

Gloria McCoy
Former President
Texas Art Education Association
Spring Branch Independent
School District, Texas

Bunyan Morris
Art Teacher
Effingham County School
System, Springfield, Georgia

Nan Yoshida
Art Education Consultant
Retired Art Supervisor
Los Angeles Unified
School District
Los Angeles, California

SRAonline.com

 SRA

Send all inquiries to:
SRA/McGraw-Hill
8787 Orion Place
Columbus, OH 43240-4027

Printed in the United States of America.

ISBN 0-07-601820-2

1 2 3 4 5 6 7 8 9 RRW 10 09 08 07 06 05 04

Contributors

Contributing Author
Jackie Ellett
Elementary Art Teacher
Duncan Creek Elementary School
Hoschton, Georgia

Artsource® Music, Dance, Theatre Lessons
Mark Slavkin, Vice President
for Education, The Music Center of
Los Angeles County
Michael Solomon, Managing Director
Music Center Education Division
Melinda Williams, Concept Originator and
Project Director
Susan Cambigue-Tracey, Project Coordinator
and Writer
Madeleine Dahm, Movement and Dance
Connection Writer
Keith Wyffels, Staff Assistance
Maureen Erbe, Logo Design

More about Aesthetics
Richard W. Burrows
Executive Director, Institute for Arts
Education
San Diego, California

Safe Use of Art Materials
Mary Ann Boykin
Director, The Art School for Children and
Young Adults
University of Houston—Clear Lake
Houston, Texas

Museum Education
Marilyn J. S. Goodman
Director of Education
Solomon R. Guggenheim Museum
New York, New York

**Resources for Students with
Disabilities**
Mandy Yeager
Ph.D. Candidate
The University of North Texas
Denton, Texas

Music Connections
Kathy Mitchell
Music Teacher
Eagan, Minnesota

Student Activities

Cassie Appleby
Glen Oaks Elementary School
McKinney, Texas

Maureen Banks
Kester Magnet School
Van Nuys, California

Christina Barnes
Webb Bridge Middle School
Alpharetta, Georgia

Beth Benning
Willis Jepson Middle School
Vacaville, California

Chad Buice
Craig Elementary School
Snellville, Georgia

Beverly Broughton
Gwinn Oaks Elementary School
Snellville, Georgia

Missy Burgess
Jefferson Elementary School
Jefferson, Georgia

Marcy Cincotta-Smith
Benefield Elementary School
Lawrenceville, Georgia

Joanne Cox
Kittredge Magnet School
Atlanta, Georgia

Carolyn Y. Craine
McCracken County Schools
Mayfield, Kentucky

Jackie Ellett
Duncan Creek Elementary School
Hoschton, Georgia

Tracie Flynn
Home School
Rushville, Indiana

Phyllis Glenn
Malcom Bridge Elementary
Bogart, Georgia

Dallas Gillespie
Dacula Middle School
Dacula, Georgia

Dr. Donald Gruber
Clinton Junior High School
Clinton, Illinois

Karen Heid
Rock Springs Elementary School
Lawrenceville, Georgia

Alisa Hyde
Southwest Elementary
Savannah, Georgia

Kie Johnson
Oconee Primary School
Watkinsville, Georgia

Sallie Keith, NBCT
West Side Magnet School
LaGrange, Georgia

Letha Kelly
Grayson Elementary School
Grayson, Georgia

Diane Kimiera
Amestoy Elementary School
Gardena, California

Desiree LaOrange
Barkley Elementary School
Fort Campbell, Kentucky

Deborah Lackey-Wilson
Roswell North Elementary
Roswell, Georgia

Dawn Laird
Goforth Elementary School
Clear Creek, Texas

Mary Lazzari
Timothy Road Elementary School
Athens, Georgia

Michelle Leonard
Webb Bridge Middle School
Alpharetta, Georgia

Lynn Ludlam
Spring Branch ISD
Houston, Texas

Mark Mitchell
Fort Daniel Elementary School
Dacula, Georgia

Martha Moore
Freeman's Mill Elementary School
Dacula, Georgia

Connie Niedenthal
Rushville Elementary
Rushville, Indiana

Barbara Patisaul
Oconee County Elementary
School
Watkinsville, Georgia

Elizabeth Paulos-Krasle
Social Circle Elementary
Social Circle, Georgia

Jane Pinneau
Rocky Branch Elementary School
Watkinsville, Georgia

Marilyn Polin
Cutler Ridge Middle School
Miami, Florida

Michael Ramsey
Graves County Schools
Paducah, Kentucky

Rosemarie Sells
Social Circle Elementary
Social Circle, Georgia

Jean Neelen Siegel
Baldwin School
California

Debra Smith
McIntosh County School System
Darien, Georgia

Patricia Spencer
Harmony Elementary School
Buford, Georgia

Melanie Stokes
Smiley Elementary School
Ludowici, Georgia

Rosanne Stutts
Davidson Fine Arts School
Augusta, Georgia

Fran Sullivan
South Jackson Elementary School
Athens, Georgia

Kathy Valentine
Home School
Burkburnett, Texas

Debi West
Rock Springs Elementary School
Lawrenceville, Georgia

Sherry White
Bauerschlog Elementary School
League City, Texas

Patricia Wiesen
Cutler Ridge Middle School
Miami, Florida

Deayna Woodruff
Loveland Middle School
Loveland, Ohio

Gil Young
Beverly Hills Middle School
Beverly Hills, California

Larry A. Young
Dacula Elementary School
Dacula, Georgia

Table of Contents

What Is Art?

About Art

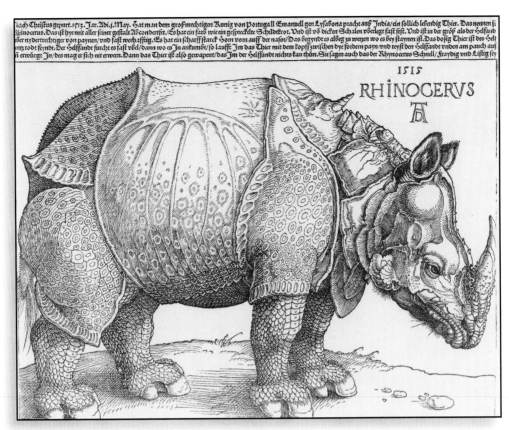

▲ **Albrecht Dürer.** *Rhinoceros.*

Unit 1 Line

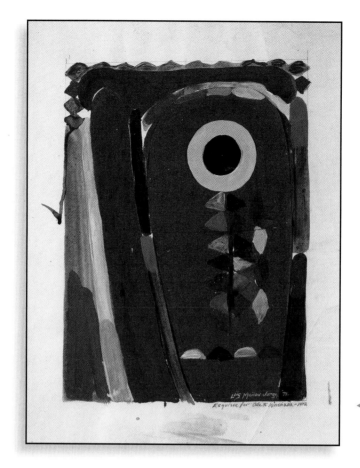

◀ **Loïs Mailou Jones.**
Esquisse for Ode to Kinshasa.

 Unit **2** Shape

6

▲ **Mary Cassatt.** *In the Garden.*

Unit 3 Color

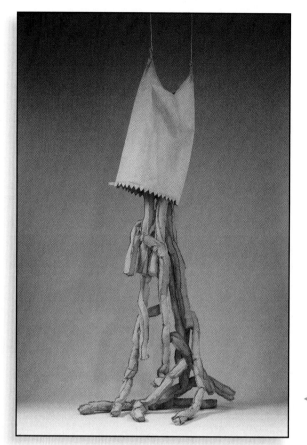

Unit 4 Form and Space

◀ **Leonardo da Vinci.**
Mona Lisa.

Unit 6 Balance, Emphasis, and Unity

Technique Tips

Activity Tips

What Is Art?

Art is . . .

Painting

▲ **Georgia O'Keeffe.** (American). *Autumn Leaves—Lake George.* 1924.

Oil on canvas. Columbus Museum of Art, Columbus, Ohio.

Drawing

▲ **Leonardo da Vinci.** (Italian). *Self Portrait.* 1514.

Red chalk, Royal Library, Turin, Italy.

Sculpture

▲ **Artist Unknown.** (Italy). *Camillus.* A.D. 41–54.

Bronze. $46\frac{7}{8}$ inches high (119.08 cm.). The Metropolitan Museum of Art, New York, New York.

Architecture

▲ **Artist Unknown.** (India). *Taj Mahal.* 1638–1648.

Marble. 240 feet tall (73.15 meters). Agra, India.

Printmaking

▲ **Katsushika Hokusai.** (Japanese). *Kirifuri Waterfall on Mt. Kurokami in Shimotsuke Province.* c. 1833–1834.

Color woodblock print. $15\frac{5}{16} \times 10\frac{3}{8}$ inches (38.9 × 26.3 cm.). Honolulu Academy of Arts, Honolulu, Hawaii.

Pottery

▲ **Harrison Mc Intosh.** (American). *Stoneware Vase #661.* 1966.

Glazed stoneware. $15\frac{1}{4} \times 13$ inches (38.74 × 33.02 cm.). Renwick Gallery, Smithsonian American Art Museum, Washington, D.C.

Weaving

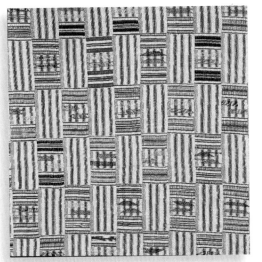

▲ **Artist Unknown.** (Ashanti Peoples, Ghana). *Kente Cloth.*

Museum of International Folk Art, Santa Fe, New Mexico.

Clothing

◀ **Artist Unknown.** (American). *Arapaho Man's Shirt.* c. 1890.

Buckskin and feathers. 37 inches (93.68 cm.) long. Buffalo Bill Historical Center, Cody, Wyoming.

Art is created by people.

What Is Art?

Every work of art has three parts.

Subject

This is the object you see in the artwork.

Composition

This is how the artwork is organized.

Content

This is what the artwork means.

▲ **W.H. Brown.** (American). *Bareback Riders.* 1886.
....
Oil on cardboard mounted on wood. $18\frac{1}{2}$ × $24\frac{1}{2}$ inches (46.99 × 61.60 cm.). National Gallery of Art, Washington, D.C.

What is the subject of this artwork?

▲ **Artist Unknown.** (Native American, Navajo). *Classic Serape Style Wearing Blanket.* 1875.

Plied cotton and Saxony wool. $73\frac{1}{2}$ × 47 inches (186.69 × 119.38 cm.). Utah Museum of Fine Arts, University of Utah, Salt Lake City, Utah.

How is this work organized?

▲ **Jacob Lawrence.** (American). *Children at Play.* 1947.

Tempera on Masonite panel. 20 × 24 inches (50.8 × 60.96 cm.). Georgia Museum of Art, University of Georgia, Athens, Georgia.

What does this artwork mean?

What Is Art?

Subject Matter

Artists make art about many subjects. Name the subjects you see on these pages.

Colors and Shapes

▲ **Auguste Herbin.** (French). *Composition on the Word "Vie" 2.* 1950.

Oil on canvas. $57\frac{1}{2} \times 38\frac{1}{4}$ inches (146.05 × 97.16 cm.). Museum of Modern Art, New York, New York.

Things Outside

▲ **Claude Monet.** (French). *The Four Trees.* 1891.

Oil on canvas. $32\frac{1}{4} \times 32\frac{1}{8}$ inches (81.92 × 81.58 cm.). The Metropolitan Museum of Art, New York, New York.

What Is Art?

Everyday Life

▲ **Carmen Lomas Garza.** (American). *Naranjas (Oranges).*

Gouache. 20 × 14 inches (50.8 × 35.56 cm.). Collection of Mr. and Mrs. Ira Schneider, Scottsdale, Arizona.

A Story

▲ **Artist Unknown.** (Hmong Peoples, Asia). *Hmong Story Cloth.*

Cotton. 18 × 18 inches (45.72 × 45.72 cm.). Private collection.

What Is Art?

People

▲ **Isabel Bishop.** (American). *Ice Cream Cones.* 1942.

Oil and egg tempera on fiberboard. $33\frac{7}{8}$ x 20 inches (86.04 x 50.8 cm.).
Museum of Fine Arts, Boston, Massachusetts.

Objects

▲ **Artist Unknown.** (Mi'kmaq People, Nova Scotia, Canada). *Letter Holder or Book Cover.*
....
Birch bark decorated with porcupine quills, glass beads, and silk. $10\frac{1}{4} \times 14\frac{1}{2}$ inches (26.04 × 36.83 cm.). Museum of International Folk Art, Santa Fe, New Mexico.

Things with a Deeper Meaning

▲ **Rufino Tamayo.** (Mexican). *Toast to the Sun.* 1956.
....
Oil on canvas. $31\frac{1}{2}$ x 39 inches (80 x 99 cm.). Wichita Art Museum, Wichita, Kansas.

Elements of Art

Art talks with . . .

Line

Shape

Form

Space

Color

Value

Texture

Principles of Art

Pattern

Rhythm

Balance

Emphasis

Harmony

Variety

Unity

About Art

▲ **Mary Cassatt.** (American). *Susan Comforting the Baby.* 1881.
Oil on canvas. $25\frac{5}{8}$ x $39\frac{3}{8}$ inches (65.1 x 100 cm.). Museum of Fine Arts, Houston, Texas.

Look at the painting.

▶ How are the people dressed?

▶ What are they doing?

▶ What can you learn about the artist?

About Art

▲ **Mary Cassatt.** (American). *Susan Comforting the Baby.* 1881.
••
Oil on canvas. $25\frac{5}{8}$ x $39\frac{3}{8}$ inches (65.1 x 100 cm.). Museum of Fine Arts, Houston, Texas.

Look

▶ Look at the work of art.
What do you see?

Look Inside

▶ Pretend you are Susan.
Tell a story about this work of art.

Look Outside

▶ What does this work make you feel?

▶ What will you remember about this
work of art?

About Art

▲ **Mary Cassatt.** (American). *Susan Comforting the Baby.* 1881.

Oil on canvas. $25\frac{5}{8}$ x $39\frac{3}{8}$ inches (65.1 x 100 cm.). Museum of Fine Arts, Houston, Texas.

 **Art Criticism**

► List the people and things you see.

Analyze

► What lines, shapes, colors, and textures do you see?

► What part stands out?

Interpret

► What is happening? What is the artist telling you about Susan and the baby?

Decide

► Have you ever seen another artwork like this?

About Art

▲ **Mary Cassatt.** (American). *Susan Comforting the Baby.* 1881.

Oil on canvas. $25\frac{5}{8}$ x $39\frac{3}{8}$ inches (65.1 x 100 cm.). Museum of Fine Arts, Houston, Texas.

 **Creative Expression**

How can you make art?

1. Get an idea.

2. Plan your work.

3. Make a sketch.

4. Use the media.

5. Share your final work.

Safety

▶ Use art materials only on your artwork.

▶ Keep art materials out of your mouth, eyes, and ears.

▶ Use only safety scissors. Keep your fingers away from the blades.

▶ Wash your hands after using the art materials.

▶ Wear an art shirt or smock to protect your clothes.

▶ Always follow your teacher's directions.

Line

▲ **Albrecht Dürer.** (German).
Rhinoceros. 1515.

Woodcut. $8\frac{3}{8} \times 11\frac{5}{8}$ inches (21.27 × 29.53 cm.). The Metropolitan Museum of Art, New York, New York.

Artists use lines in their works of art.

This picture of a rhinoceros has many lines.

Look at the picture.

▶ Where do you see lines that go up and down?

▶ Where do you see lines that are leaning?

▶ Where do you see lines that go from side to side?

In This Unit you will:

▶ learn about different kinds of lines.

▶ find lines in art and the environment.

▶ create art with lines.

Self-Portrait

Albrecht Dürer

(1471–1528)

▶ was a German artist.

▶ made paintings, drawings, and prints.

▶ created art about many subjects.

Lines

Look at the works of art on these pages. The artists used many kinds of lines to create the paintings.

▲ **Joaquín Torres-García.** (Uruguayan). *New York City– Bird's-Eye View.* c. 1920.

Gouache and watercolor on board. $13\frac{1}{2} \times 19\frac{1}{2}$ inches (34.29 × 49.53 cm.). Yale University Art Gallery, New Haven, Connecticut.

Art History and Culture

At the time these works were painted, many artists were making abstract art. Abstract art does not show objects the way they really look.

▲ **Wassily Kandinsky.** (Russian).
Composition 8. 1923.
Oil on canvas. $55\frac{1}{8} \times 79\frac{1}{8}$ inches
(140×201 cm.). Solomon R. Guggenheim
Museum, New York, New York.

Study both works of art to find lines.

▶ Can you find thick, thin, smooth, rough, solid, and broken lines?

Aesthetic Perception

Seeing Like an Artist Look around. Can you find lines like those in the paintings?

Using Lines

A **line** is a mark made by an artist's tool as it moves. Here are different kinds of lines:

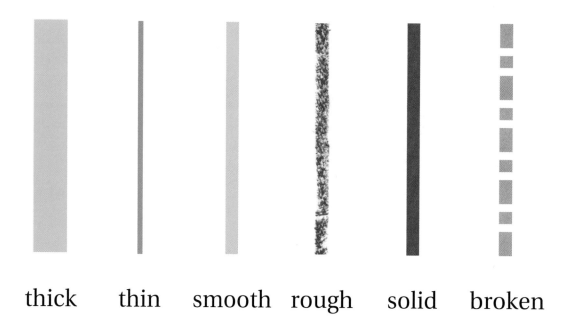

thick   thin   smooth   rough   solid   broken

Practice

Make different lines with your classmates.

1. Line up in single file to make a thin line.
2. Line up in pairs to make a thick line.
3. Can you make other lines?

▲ **Ty Brannen.** Age 7.

Think about how this student used lines.

 **Creative Expression**

How many different ways can you use lines?

1. Think of a design you can make with thick, thin, smooth, rough, solid, and broken lines.

2. Fill your paper with lines.

3. Brush watercolor paint over your lines.

Art Criticism

Analyze What kinds of lines did you use? Did you fill your paper?

Look at the paintings on these pages. These paintings look calm and quiet.

◀ **Wolf Kahn.** (American).
Lilac-colored Landscape. 1998.
....
Oil on canvas. 40 × 42 inches
(101.6 × 106.7 cm.). Thomas Segal Gallery,
Baltimore, Maryland.

🏺 Art History and Culture

These artists made paintings to show their feelings. How do you think they felt about the world around them?

▲ **Piet Mondrian.** (Dutch). *Composition V.* 1914.

Oil on canvas. $21\frac{5}{8} \times 33\frac{5}{8}$ inches (54.93 × 85.41 cm.). The Museum of Modern Art, New York, New York.

Study both works of art to find different lines.

▶ Which ways do the lines go?

Aesthetic Perception

Design Awareness Look around. What objects have calm lines?

Using Calm Lines

vertical

horizontal

Artists use **vertical** and **horizontal** lines to make a picture look calm.

Calm lines are used to make a **landscape,** or picture of the outdoors.

Practice

Use your body to make calm lines.

1. Stand straight like a vertical line. Stand as tall as you can.
2. Lie on the ground like a horizontal line. Be very still.
3. Did you feel calm when you made each kind of line?

▲ **Anna Pofer.** Age 7.

Think about how this student used calm lines.

 **Creative Expression**

How can you show your favorite quiet outdoor place?

1. Start your landscape with calm lines.

2. You can add other lines to complete your picture.

3. Fill the page.

Art Criticism

Interpret What season did you show? How can you tell?

▲ **Jasper Johns.** (American). *Between the Clock and the Bed.* 1981.

Encaustic. $6\frac{1}{8} \times 10\frac{3}{4}$ inches (15.56 × 27.31 cm.). The Museum of Modern Art, New York, New York.

Look at the works of art on these pages. The diagonal lines make your eyes move around the page.

Art History and Culture

Jasper Johns got the idea for this painting from a pattern he saw in another painting.

◀ **Sylvia Plimack Mangold.** (American). *The Elm Tree (Summer).* 1991.

Oil on linen. 80 × 60 inches (203.2 × 152.4 cm.). Alexander and Bonin, New York, New York.

Study both works of art.

▶ Where do you see diagonal lines?

Aesthetic Perception

Seeing Like an Artist Look around. Where do you see diagonal lines?

Using Diagonal Lines

diagonal

Diagonal lines are slanted. They give artwork a busy feeling.

zigzag

Zigzag lines are made by connecting diagonal lines.

Practice

Use your body to make diagonal lines.

1. Pretend you are a tree. Your arms will make the branches.
2. Hold up your arms away from your body. Make them look like diagonal lines.
3. Spread your fingers apart to make thin branches.

Think about how this student used diagonal lines.

◄ **Peyton Wilker.** Age 6.

Creative Expression

How could you show tree branches that grew in many different directions?

1. Think about how a tree changes as it grows.

2. Tear a sheet of paper to make a tree trunk. Tear thick branches and thin branches. Tear leaves.

3. Glue your tree onto another sheet of paper.

 **Art Criticism**

Decide Do the diagonal lines make your eyes move all around your picture?

Lesson 4 · Curved Lines

▲ **Agnes Tait.** (American).
Skating in Central Park. 1934.

Oil on canvas. $33\frac{7}{8} \times 48\frac{1}{8}$ inches (86.04 × 122.24 cm.). Smithsonian American Art Museum, Washington, D.C.

Look at the works of art on these pages. The curved lines make your eyes move gently around the page.

🏺 Art History and Culture

Bridal Bed Cover was made for a newly married couple. Each picture on the bedcover has a special meaning.

Study both works of art.

► Where do you see curved lines?

Aesthetic Perception

Design Awareness Look around for curved lines. Where do you see them?

Using Curved Lines

Curved lines bend. They change direction slowly.

Practice

Draw the lines a figure skater makes on ice.

1. Think about a figure skater moving gracefully across the ice.

2. Pretend your marker is the skater. Pretend your paper is the ice. Move your marker and draw the lines.

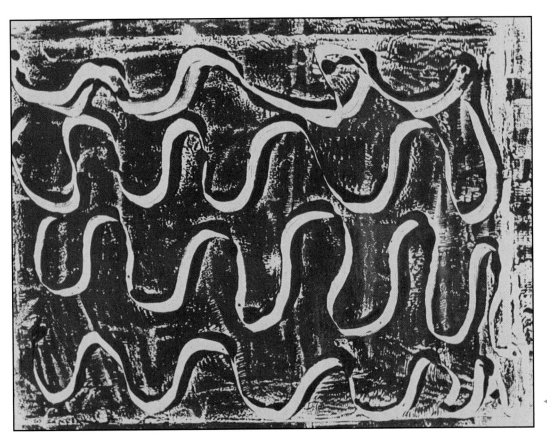

◀ **Marcus Ellis.**
Age 6.

Think about how this student used curved lines.

 **Creative Expression**

How can you make a print of curved lines?

1. Tape a square of plastic wrap to the table. Spread paint on it.

2. Pull a comb through the paint to make curved lines. Use gentle movement.

3. Lay paper on top of the paint to make a print.

Art Criticism

Decide If you made the artwork again, what would you change?

Buildings Have Lines

▲ **Lawren S. Harris.**
(Canadian). *Shacks.*
1919.
. . . .
Oil on canvas. $42\frac{1}{2} \times 50\frac{3}{8}$
inches (107.9 × 128 cm.).
National Gallery of Canada,
Ottawa, Ontario, Canada.

Look at the works of art on these pages.
The artists used lines to make buildings.

Art History and Culture

Do the buildings in these works of art look like
buildings you might see in your neighborhood
today?

Study both works of art to find lines.

▶ What lines did each artist use to
make the buildings?

Aesthetic Perception

Design Awareness Look at your school building.
Can you find lines like those you saw in the works
of art?

Using Lines to Make Buildings

Artists use vertical, horizontal, and diagonal lines to make pictures of **buildings.**

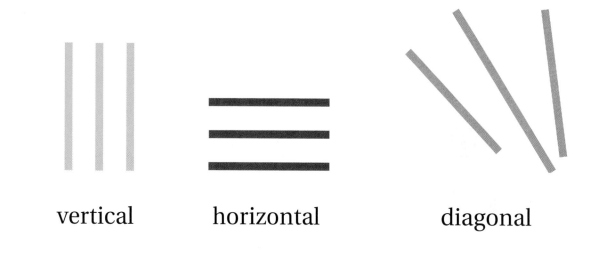

vertical   horizontal   diagonal

Practice

Draw different parts of buildings.

1. Think of parts that most buildings have.
2. Draw the parts with chalk on black construction paper.
3. Notice the lines you used.

Think about how this student used lines to make a building.

◀ **Tricia Scott.** Age 6.

 **Creative Expression**

What could you use to make the lines of a building?

1. Start with a piece of cardboard for the building.

2. Use different objects to add parts to the building. Add windows, doors, and a roof.

3. What else can you add to make the building unique?

Art Criticism

Interpret Who would use a building like the one you made?

Lines Show Movement

▲ **Jacob Lawrence.**
(American).
Children at Play.
1947.
....
Tempera on Masonite
panel. 20 × 24 inches
(50.8 × 60.96 cm.).
Georgia Museum of Art,
University of Georgia,
Athens, Georgia.

Look at the works of art on these pages.
The artists used active lines to show people
and animals moving.

🏺 Art History and Culture

Harrison Begay was a Native American artist. He
painted pictures of traditional Navajo activities.

▲ **Harrison Begay.** (Native American, Navajo). *Night Chant Ceremonial Hunt.* 1947.

Watercolor on paper. 20 × 30 inches (50.8 × 76.2 cm.). The Philbrook Museum of Art, Tulsa, Oklahoma.

Study both works of art.

▶ What things are moving?

▶ What kinds of lines do those things have?

🔍 Aesthetic Perception

Seeing Like an Artist Look around. Do you see anything with active lines?

Using Lines to Show Movement

Diagonal, zigzag, and curved lines are active lines. They are used to show movement.

diagonal

zigzag

curved

Practice

Show movement with your classmates.

1. Think of a game or sport you like to play.

2. Pretend to play the game. Stop when your teacher says, "Freeze!"

3. Look at the lines made by your classmates' arms and legs.

Think about how this student showed movement.

Creative Expression

How can you show the movement you make when you play?

1. Think about the lines that show this movement.

2. Use the brush tool in your computer's paint program to draw yourself at play.

3. Fill the page.

Art Criticism

Describe What are you doing in the picture? Tell about the game you are playing.

Line

▲ **Joseph Norman.** (American).
Spanish Garden #IV. 1994–1995.

Acrylic on paper. 50 × 40 inches (127 × 101.6 cm.).
Private collection.

Art Criticism · Critical Thinking

Describe

▶ What objects do you see in this painting?

Analyze

▶ Where do you see thick lines in this painting?

Interpret

▶ Do the lines make this work look busy or calm?

Decide

▶ Is this a realistic painting?

Show What You Know

Write your answers on a sheet of paper.

1 Choose the thick line.

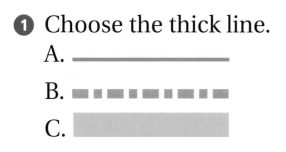

A.

B.

C.

2 Which lines are not calm lines?

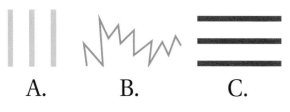

A.   B.   C.

3 Which lines show movement?

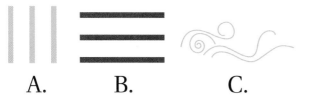

A.   B.   C.

LET'S VISIT A MUSEUM
Telfair Museum of Art

This museum is in Savannah, Georgia. It is the oldest art museum in the South. The museum's collection is located in a mansion that used to be the home of the Telfair family.

Lines in Song Writing

A songwriter writes lines for songs. The lines are made up of words. Sometimes the lines rhyme.

What to Do Write two rhyming lines about an endangered animal.

1. Listen to Paul Tracey's song about endangered animals. Talk about what the lines of the song mean.

2. Work in a group. Choose an endangered animal. Write two lines about why the animal is special.

3. Read or sing your lines for others.

▲ **Paul Tracey. "Our Little Blue Planet."**

Describe What did you learn about writing lines for a song?

Shape

◀ **Loïs Mailou Jones.**
(American). *Esquisse for Ode to Kinshasa.* 1972.
• • • • • • • • • • • • • • •
Acrylic on paper.
11 × 8 inches
(27.9 × 91.4 cm.). The National Museum of Women in the Arts, Washington, D.C.

Artists use shapes in their works of art.

This artwork has many shapes.

A **shape** is created by the line all around it.

▶ What shapes can you find in the artwork?

▶ What kinds of lines make each shape?

In This Unit you will:

▶ learn about geometric and free-form shapes.

▶ find shapes in art and the environment.

▶ create art with shapes.

Loïs Mailou Jones
(1905–1998)

▶ was an American artist.

▶ made paintings.

▶ used African themes.

Lines Outline Shapes

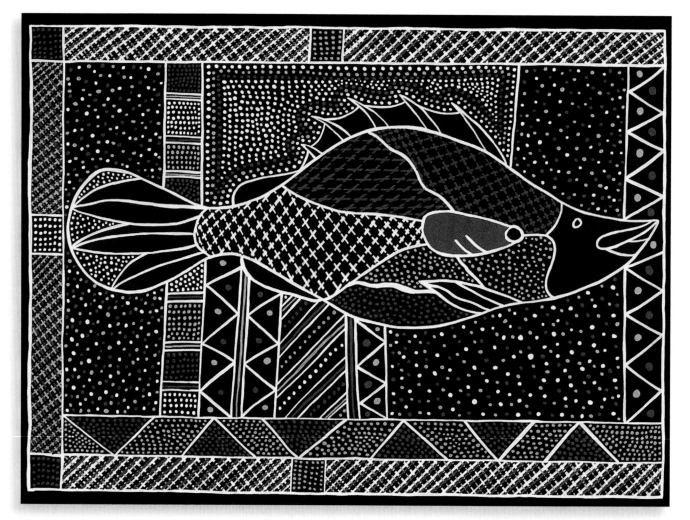

Look at the works of art on these pages. The artists used lines to make animal shapes.

▲ **Francesca Puruntatameri.** (Australian). *Muniti Red Snapper.* c. 1998.

Gouache on paper. 20 × 28 inches (50.8 × 71.12 cm.). Private collection.

Art History and Culture

Deborah Butterfield only makes art about horses! She often uses found materials in her horse sculptures.

▲ **Deborah Butterfield.**
(American). *Rex.* 1991.
....
Found, painted steel. 77 × 110
× 24 inches (195.58 × 279.4
× 60.96 cm.). Lowe Art
Museum, Coral Gables, Florida.

Study both works of art to find shapes.

▶ What kinds of lines make the shapes?

Aesthetic Perception

Seeing Like an Artist Find an object near you.
Trace its outline.

Using Lines to Outline Shapes

Shapes are made when lines come together. A line around the edge of a shape is its **outline.**

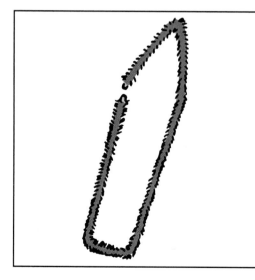

Practice making outlines.

1. Choose an object in the classroom.
2. Trace the outline of the shape with your finger.
3. Bend a chenille stem to make the outline.

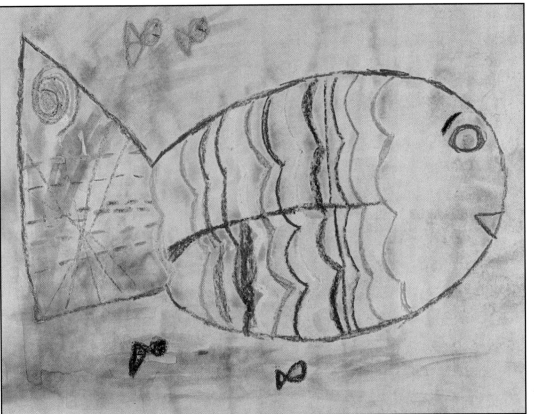

◀ **Tori Hatten.**
Age 6.

Think about how this student used lines to outline shapes.

 **Creative Expression**

What shapes would you put in an ocean scene?

1. Use crayons to draw outlines of fish shapes and plant shapes.

2. Use big shapes, medium-sized shapes, and small shapes.

3. Brush watercolor over your page.

Art Criticism

Interpret Is your ocean a friendly place or a scary place? How can you tell?

Geometric Shapes

Look at the paintings on these pages. The artists used geometric shapes in their works of art.

◄ **Auguste Herbin.** (French).
Vie No. 1 (Life No. 1). 1950.

Oil on canvas. 57 × 38 inches (144.78 × 96.52 cm.). Albright-Knox Art Gallery, Buffalo, New York.

Art History and Culture

Le Pont Saint-Michel in Paris shows a real place. The artist lived near the river. He made many paintings of it.

▲ **Albert Marquet.** (French).
Le Pont Saint-Michel in Paris.
1908.

Oil on canvas. $25\frac{5}{8} \times 31\frac{7}{8}$ inches
(65.09 × 80.96 cm.). The State
Pushkin Museum, Moscow, Russia.

Study both works of art to find geometric shapes.

► What shapes can you name?

Aesthetic Perception

Design Awareness Look around. Do you see any geometric shapes?

Using Geometric Shapes

Some shapes are **geometric shapes.**

Geometric shapes have names.

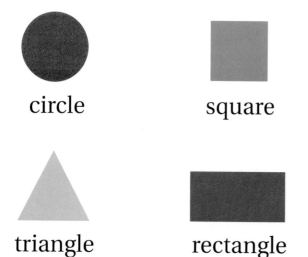

circle   square

triangle   rectangle

Practice

Find objects that look like geometric shapes.

1. Form a group with other students.

2. Look around the classroom for objects with the shape your teacher tells you.

3. Count the objects your group finds.

Lauren Faske.
Age 6.

Think about how this student used geometric shapes.

 **Creative Expression**

How could you arrange geometric shapes to make a picture?

1. Make texture rubbings on paper.

2. Trace the outlines of geometric shapes on the paper.

3. Cut out the shapes. Arrange them to make a design. Glue the shapes to black paper.

Art Criticism

Analyze Which colors and shapes look the most important? Why?

Free-Form Shapes

Look at the shapes of the animals and the leaves. The shape of a living thing is a free-form shape.

◄ **Henri Rousseau.**
(French).
The Equatorial Jungle.
1909.
....
Oil on canvas. $55\frac{1}{4}$ × 51 inches
(140.6 × 129.5 cm.). National
Gallery of Art, Washington, D.C.

Art History and Culture

Henri Rousseau never went to the jungle, but he painted many jungle scenes. He got his ideas from reading books and visiting the zoo.

Hung Liu. (Chinese American). *Hong Shancha: Red Camellia.* 2002.

Oil on canvas. 60 × 48 inches (152.4 × 121.92 cm.). Bernice Steinbaum Gallery, Miami, Florida.

Study both works of art to find free-form shapes.

▶ What free-form shapes do you see?

Aesthetic Perception

Seeing Like an Artist Look around. What things can you find that have free-form shapes?

Using Free-Form Shapes

Free-form shapes are not geometric shapes.

Practice

Look for free-form shapes in magazines.

1. Look for pictures of living things.
2. Can you find other free-form shapes?

Think about how this student used a free-form shape.

◀ **Jensen Palmer.** Age 7.

Creative Expression

What free-form shapes did you find?

1. Sketch a free-form shape you found in a magazine.

2. Go over the lines with black glue.

3. When the glue is dry, color your picture with pastels.

Art Criticism

Analyze What kinds of lines did you use to make your shape?

People Shapes

Look at the paintings on these pages. The artists used free-form shapes to paint people.

◀ **Carmen Lomas Garza.**
(American). *Naranjas (Oranges).*
Gouache. 20 × 14 inches (50.8 × 35.56 cm.).
Collection of Mr. and Mrs. Ira Schneider,
Scottsdale, Arizona.

Art History and Culture

Carmen Lomas Garza makes art to show things she did with her family when she was a child.

Study both works of art.

▶ What people shapes do you see?

▶ What other free-form shapes do you see?

◀ **Isabel Bishop.** (American). *Ice Cream Cones.* 1942.

· ·

Oil and egg tempera on fiberboard. $33\frac{7}{8} \times 20$ inches (86.04 × 50.8 cm.). Museum of Fine Arts, Boston, Massachusetts.

Aesthetic Perception

Seeing Like an Artist Trace in the air the outline of a classmate. What kind of shape did you make?

Using People Shapes

The human body is a **free-form shape.**

It is made of smaller free-form shapes.

Draw the free-form shapes of different body parts.

1. Use your finger to trace the outline of a body part, such as your head, ear, or foot.

2. Draw the shape of the outline you traced.

◀ **Jesse Drewa.** Age 7.

Think about how this student made the shape of a person.

 **Creative Expression**

What does the free-form shape of your body look like?

1. Lie on a large piece of paper.

2. Have a partner trace the outline of your body.

3. Paint your portrait with tempera paints.

Art Criticism

Describe What are you wearing in your portrait?

Shapes of People in Action

Look at the shapes of the people in these paintings. Notice the position of each person's arms and legs.

◀ **Jacob Lawrence.** (American). *Builders—Red and Green Ball.* 1979.

Gouache on paper. 30 × 22 inches (76.2 × 55.88 cm.). Courtesy of the artist and Francine Seders Gallery LTD., Seattle, Washington.

Art History and Culture

Jacob Lawrence painted with an abstract style. Janet Fish paints with a realistic style.

▲ **Janet Fish.** (American).
Jump. 1995.
....
Oil on canvas. 54 × 70 inches
(137.16 × 177.8 cm.). D.C. Moore
Gallery, New York, New York.

Study both works of art to find
people in action.

▶ What are the people doing?

▶ How can you tell?

Aesthetic Perception

Seeing Like an Artist Move one hand in the air.
How does the shape of your hand change?

Using Shapes of People in Action

Changing the **position** of body parts can show how people move.

Practice

Demonstrate movement to your classmates.

1. Decide on a game or sport that you like to play.

2. Pretend to play the game.

3. Have other classmates guess what you are doing. How did they know?

◀ **Heather Faulkner.** Age 6.

Think about how this student showed herself in action.

Creative Expression

How can you show how you move when you play?

1. Think about what your body looks like when you play your favorite game.

2. Draw yourself at play. Use action shapes to show how you move.

Art Criticism

Decide Did you use free-form shapes to show body movement?

Still-Life Shapes

▲ **Paul Cézanne.** (French). *Still Life with Apples and Peaches.* c. 1905.

Oil on canvas. 32 × 39⅝ inches (81 × 100.5 cm.). National Gallery of Art, Washington, D.C.

Look at the still lifes on these pages. A still life is a picture of things that do not move.

🏺 **Art History and Culture**

Many artists paint still lifes. How are these still lifes similar? How are they different?

◄ **Pablo Picasso.**
(Spanish). *The Red Foulard.* 1924.
....
Oil on canvas. 39½ × 32 inches (100.33 × 81.28 cm.). Norton Museum of Art, West Palm Beach, Florida.

Study both works of art to find shapes.

▶ What shapes were used in each painting?

Aesthetic Perception

Design Awareness Look for a still life at home. Is there a plant or a bowl of fruit on a table?

Using Still-Life Shapes

A **still life** has **geometric** and **free-form shapes.**

Arrange objects that could be used in a still life.

1. Use five objects you find in the classroom.

2. Arrange the objects on a table.

3. What shapes do you see?

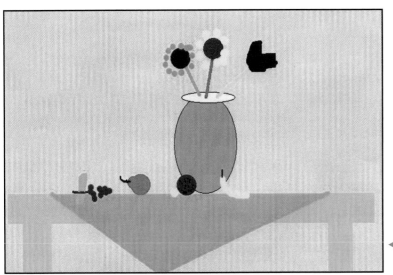

Think about how this student used geometric and free-form shapes to make a still life.

🎨 Creative Expression

What objects would you place in a still life?

1. Choose your objects. Decide how you would arrange them.

2. Use the shape tools in your computer's paint program to draw objects with geometric shapes. Use the brush tool to draw objects with free-form shapes.

3. Use the fill tool to paint the objects. Use other tools to decorate your picture.

⚠️❓ Art Criticism

Decide If you made another still life, what objects would you include?

Shape

▲ **Pierre Bonnard.** (French). *The Breakfast Room.*
1930-1931.

Oil on canvas. $62\frac{7}{8} \times 44\frac{7}{8}$ inches (159.3 × 113.8 cm.). The Museum of Modern Art, New York, New York.

Critical Thinking

Describe

▶ Describe the room and the objects in it.

Analyze

▶ Where do you see geometric shapes?

Interpret

▶ What sounds would you hear if you were in this room?

Decide

▶ Would you like to be in this room? Explain your answer.

Show What You Know

Write your answers on a sheet of paper.

1 Choose the free-form shape.

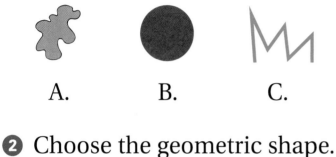

A.   B.   C.

2 Choose the geometric shape.

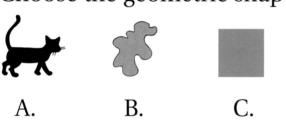

A.   B.   C.

3 Choose the shape that shows a person in action.

A.   B.   C.

Fashion Design

Think about clothing. What different kinds of shirts have you seen? Does your clothing have any patterns on the fabric?

Fashion designers plan what pieces of clothing will look like. They think of ways to change styles or make new styles of the clothes people wear.

Fabric designers create the patterns that appear on fabric.

▲ **Fashion designer**

Shape in Theatre

An artist creates shapes and images on paper. When these pictures go with a story, they are called illustrations. Sometimes a theatre director makes a play using the story and illustrations from a book.

What to Do Re-create a scene from an illustration in a book.

1. Choose an illustration that shows characters in action.

2. Work in a group. Use your bodies to show the poses of the characters.

3. Share your scene with the other groups.

▲ The Children's Theatre Company. "The Story of Babar."

 **Art Criticism**

Decide Did your group bring the illustration from the page to the stage?

Color

▲ **Mary Cassatt.** (American).
In the Garden. 1904.

Pastel. 26 × 32 inches (66 × 81.3 cm.).
The Detroit Institute of Arts, Detroit,
Michigan.

Artists use many colors in their works of art.

They mix some colors to make other colors.

Look at the artwork.

▶ What colors do you see?

In This Unit you will:

▶ learn about the color wheel, primary colors, and secondary colors.

▶ find colors in art and the environment.

▶ create art with primary and secondary colors.

Mary Cassatt

(1844–1926)

▶ was an American artist.

▶ often painted mothers and their children.

▶ used paint and pastels.

A Rainbow of Colors

Look at the works of art on these pages. The artists used the colors of the rainbow.

Art History and Culture

Ellsworth Kelly also painted *Spectrum II.* It is identical to *Spectrum III* but more than eight times bigger.

Study the works of art.

▶ What colors do you see?

▲ **David Hockney.** (British).
Hollywood Hills House. 1982.
. . . .
Oil, charcoal, collage on canvas. Three panels,
60 × 120 inches (152.4 × 304.8 cm.) overall.
Walker Art Center, Minneapolis, Minnesota.

Aesthetic Perception

Design Awareness Find something in the room
that matches each color of the rainbow.

Using a Rainbow of Colors

A **color wheel** shows the colors of the **rainbow** in order.

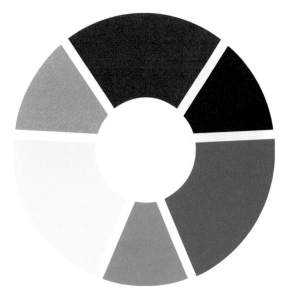

Practice

Make a color wheel.

1. Look in an old magazine.

2. Find and cut out pictures for all colors in the color wheel.

3. Glue the pictures in the order of the color wheel.

▲ **Andrea Waldon.**
Age 6.

Think about how this student used rainbow colors.

How would you change the colors of things around you?

1. Think of objects you would like to make colorful. Draw the outlines of the objects with a black marker.

2. Using crayons, color the objects with rainbow colors in order.

3. Paint the background with rainbow colors in order.

 **Art Criticism**

Describe Which objects did you draw?

Primary Colors

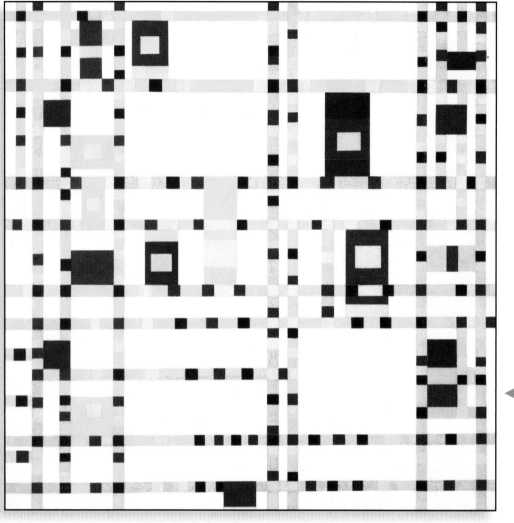

◀ **Piet Mondrian.**
(Dutch). *Broadway Boogie-Woogie.*
1942–1943.

. . . .

Oil on canvas. 50 × 50 inches (127 × 127 cm.). The Museum of Modern Art, New York, New York.

Look at the paintings on these pages.
They have primary colors.

🏺 Art History and Culture

These artists formed groups with other artists who had similar styles and similar ideas about art.

▲ **Selden Connor Gile.** (American).
Two Fishermen and a Boat. c. 1917.
Oil on panel. 15 × 18 inches (38.1 × 45.72 cm.).
Norton Museum of Art, Palm Beach, Florida.

Study the works of art.

► What colors do you see?

Aesthetic Perception

Design Awareness What color is a fire engine?
A police uniform? A school bus?

Using Primary Colors

Red, yellow, and blue are **primary colors.**

Practice

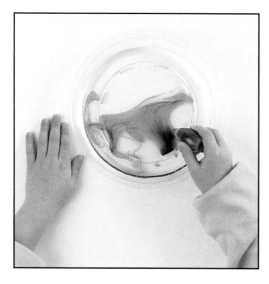

Try to mix food coloring to make primary colors.

1. Add drops of food coloring to water. Add drops of another color.

2. Try to make red, yellow, or blue.

3. Did it work?

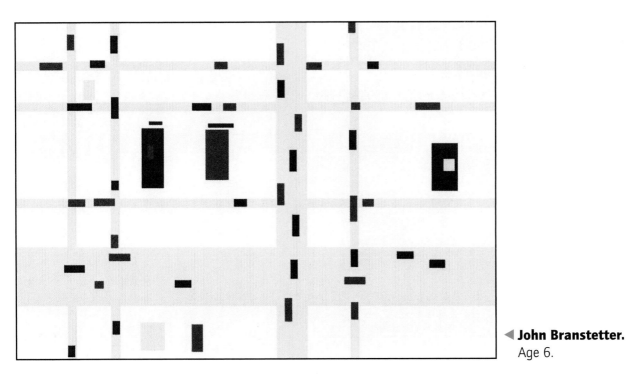

Think about how this student used primary colors.

Creative Expression

How could you show what a city looks like from above?

1. Use the computer's paint program. Choose a primary color to draw horizontal and vertical lines that represent streets.

2. Use the other primary colors to draw lines that represent cars and trucks on the streets.

3. Draw primary-colored shapes to represent buildings in the white space.

Art Criticism

Interpret What feeling does your picture create? Give it a title.

Red and Yellow Make Orange

◀ **Artist Unknown.**
(Ecuador). *Man's Headband of Toucan Feathers.*
. . . .
Cotton, feathers, human hair, and thread. Courtesy of the Smithsonian National Museum of the American Indian, New York, New York.

Look at the colors in these works of art.
The artists used red, yellow, and orange.

Art History and Culture

Rufino Tamayo usually liked to use only two or three colors in a painting.

▲ **Rufino Tamayo.** (Mexican).
Toast to the Sun. 1956.
Oil on canvas. $31\frac{1}{2} \times 39$ inches (80 × 99 cm.).
Wichita Art Museum, Wichita, Kansas.

Study the works of art.

▶ Where do you see red?

▶ Where do you see yellow?

▶ Where do you see orange?

Aesthetic Perception

Design Awareness Look around. Do you see anything orange?

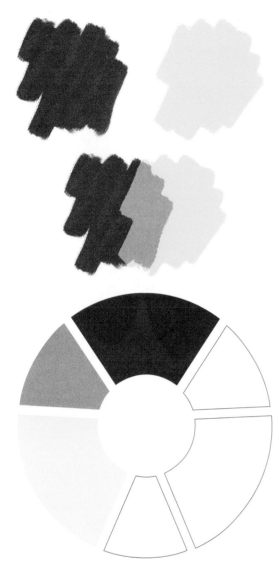

Using Red and Yellow to Make Orange

Red and yellow are **primary colors.** They can be mixed to make the **secondary color** orange.

Orange is between red and yellow on the color wheel.

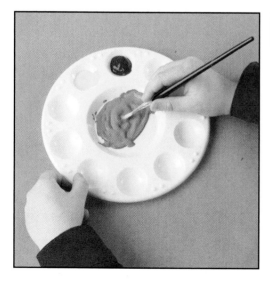

Practice

Mix red and yellow to make orange.

1. Start with yellow paint. Add red. Mix to make orange.

2. Try adding more red. How did the color change?

3. See how many oranges you can make.

◄ **Amy Kuhn.** Age 5.

Think about how this student used red, yellow, and orange.

How many different oranges can you make using only yellow and red?

1. Think of a shape for yellow and one for red. Paint your shapes.

2. Mix red and yellow paint to make orange. See how many oranges you can make.

3. Fill the rest of the paper with orange.

Art Criticism

Analyze How many different oranges did you create and paint?

Blue and Yellow Make Green

▲ **Ivan Eyre.** (Canadian). *Touchwood Hills.* 1972–1973.

Acrylic on canvas. 58 × 65 inches (147.3 × 167.6 cm.). National Gallery of Canada, Ottawa, Ontario.

Look at the works of art on these pages. The artists used blue, yellow, and green.

Art History and Culture

Many artists paint landscapes showing their surroundings.

108 Unit 3 • Lesson 4

◀ **Georgia O'Keeffe.**
(American). *Papaw Tree—'Iao Valley.*
1939.
Oil on canvas. 19 × 16 inches (48.3 × 40.6 cm.). Honolulu Academy of Arts, Honolulu, Hawaii.

Study both works of art.

▶ How many greens do you see?

Aesthetic Perception

Seeing Like an Artist Collect some green leaves. Arrange them from lightest to darkest green.

Using Blue and Yellow to Make Green

Blue and yellow are **primary colors.** They can be mixed to make the **secondary color** green.

Green is between yellow and blue on the color wheel.

Practice

Mix blue and yellow to make green.

1. Use a blue oil pastel to make a shape on paper.

2. Cover the shape with yellow pastel. Blend the colors.

3. Make another shape with yellow pastel. Then cover it with blue pastel. Blend the colors.

4. Which green is stronger?

Think about how this student made
a green scene.

Creative Expression

What colors do you see most
outdoors? Draw a green scene.

1. Imagine a summer day outside.
   Choose the green things to put
   in your scene.

2. Make green things by mixing
   blue and yellow.

3. Use blue and yellow to fill the
   background.

Art Criticism

Describe What objects
did you draw?

Red and Blue Make Violet

▲ **Grace Hartigan.**
(American). *Dido.* 1960.
. . . .
Oil on canvas. 82 × 91 inches
(208.28 × 231.14 cm.). McNay
Art Museum, San Antonio, Texas.

Look at the works of art on these pages.
The artists used red, blue, and violet.

🏺 Art History and Culture

Henri Matisse was the leader of a group of artists
called the Fauves. *Fauves* means "wild beasts" in
French.

Study the paintings.

▶ Where do you see red?

▶ Where do you see blue?

▶ Where do you see violet?

◀ **Henri Matisse.** (French).
A Glimpse of Notre Dame in the Late Afternoon. 1902.
∙∙∙∙∙∙∙∙∙∙∙∙∙∙∙∙∙∙∙∙∙∙∙∙∙∙∙∙∙∙∙
Oil on paper mounted on canvas.
$28\frac{1}{2} \times 21\frac{1}{2}$ inches (72.39 × 54.61 cm.).
Albright-Knox Art Gallery, Buffalo, New York.

Aesthetic Perception

Design Awareness Look around your classroom. What do you see that is violet?

Using Red and Blue to Make Violet

Red and blue are **primary colors.** They can be mixed to make the **secondary color** violet.

Violet is between blue and red on the color wheel.

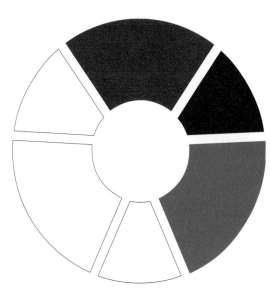

Mix red and blue to create violet.

1. Place red tissue paper on top of blue.

2. Hold the tissue paper up to the light to see the colors mix.

3. Try pink and light blue or dark red and dark blue. See how many different violet colors you can create.

◄ **Payton Myers.**
Age 7.

Think about how this student used blue and red to make violet.

What would a violet creature look like?

1. Overlap torn pieces of red and blue tissue paper.

2. Glue the tissue paper to a sheet of white paper to make the shape of your creature.

3. Add details to your creature with black marker.

Art Criticism

Interpret Is your creature scary or nice? How can you tell?

Primary and Secondary Colors

◄ **Thomas Hart Benton.**
(American). *July Hay.* 1943.

Oil and egg tempera on composition
board. 38 × 26¾ inches (96.52 × 67.95 cm.).
Metropolitan Museum of Art, New York,
New York.

Look at the colors
in these works of
art. The artists
used primary and
secondary colors.

Art History and Culture

These artists painted *genre* paintings. A genre
painting shows scenes of everyday life.

▲ **Maurice Prendergast.**
(Canadian/American).
Summer, New England. 1912.

Oil on canvas. $19\frac{1}{4} \times 27\frac{1}{2}$ inches (48.9 × 69.9 cm.).
Smithsonian American Art Museum,
Washington, D.C.

Study the colors in the paintings.

▶ What primary colors do you see?

▶ What secondary colors do you see?

Aesthetic Perception

Seeing Like an Artist Name things in your room with primary colors. Name things with secondary colors.

Using Primary and Secondary Colors

The three **primary colors** can be used to create three **secondary colors.**

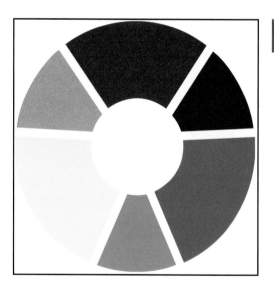

Practice

Review primary and secondary colors.

1. Form a group with some classmates.

2. Use the color flash cards. Take turns naming the colors.

3. Tell which primary colors make each secondary color.

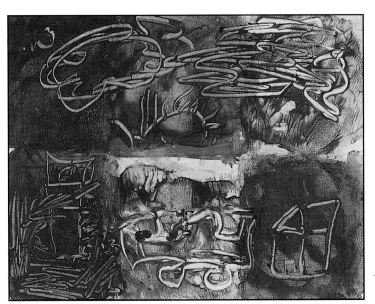

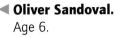
◀ **Oliver Sandoval.**
Age 6.

Think about how this student used primary and secondary colors.

🎨 **Creative Expression**

What kinds of things do you see during summer in your neighborhood?

1. Fold your paper in half. On one half, paint squares of each primary color. On the other half, paint squares of the primary color needed to make each secondary color.

2. Fold your paper and press to mix the paint.

3. Use craft sticks to draw your scene in the wet paint.

Describe What does your painting show?

Color

▲ **Hans Hofmann.** (German/American).
Au Printemps, Springtime. 1955.

Oil on canvas. 48 × 36 inches (121.92 × 91.44 cm.). Frances
Lehman Loeb Art Center, Vassar College, Poughkeepsie, New York.

Describe

▶ Describe what you see in the painting.

Analyze

▶ What colors from the color wheel do you see in this painting?

Interpret

▶ Is this a calm or busy picture? Why?

Decide

▶ Would you like to have this painting in your classroom? Why or why not?

Show What You Know

Write your answers on a sheet of paper.

1 Which is not a primary color?

A.   B.   C.

2 Which is not a secondary color?

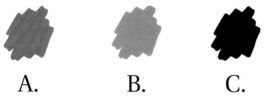

A.   B.   C.

3 Which color combination is not correct?

A.   B.   C.

LET'S VISIT A MUSEUM

Frances Lehman Loeb Art Center

This museum is located at Vassar College in Poughkeepsie, New York. The collection has over 15,000 pieces. It has art from ancient times to the present.

Color in Chinese Dance

Lily Cai performs traditional Chinese ribbon dancing. She moves through space to create patterns with the red ribbons.

What to Do Create a colorful ribbon dance.

1. Choose a color for your ribbon stick. Practice using the ribbon stick. Use full body movements.

2. Choose different movements to create a dance.

3. Perform your ribbon dance with others.

▲ **Lily Cai. "Flying Goddess."**

Art Criticism

Interpret What feeling did your ribbon dance have?

Form and Space

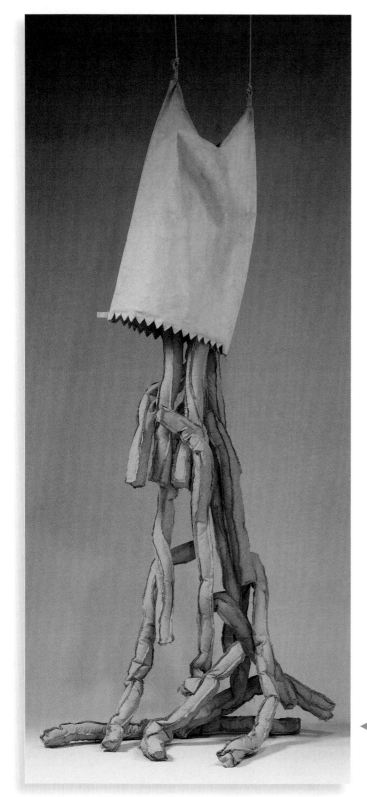

Artists create forms that take up space.

This artwork has forms that hang from the ceiling to the floor.

◀ **Claes Oldenburg.** (American). *Shoestring Potatoes Spilling from a Bag.* 1966.

Canvas, kapok, glue, acrylic. 108 × 46 × 42 inches (274.32 × 116.84 × 106.68 cm.). Walker Art Center, Minneapolis, Minnesota.

A **form** has height, width, and depth. **Space** is all around it.

Look at the artwork.
▶ What forms do you see?
▶ Where do you see space?

In This Unit you will:
▶ learn about form and space.
▶ find form and space in art and the environment.
▶ create art with form and space.

Claes Oldenburg
(1929 –)

▶ is an American artist.
▶ creates sculptures of everyday objects.
▶ sculpts objects much larger than they really are.

Shapes and Forms

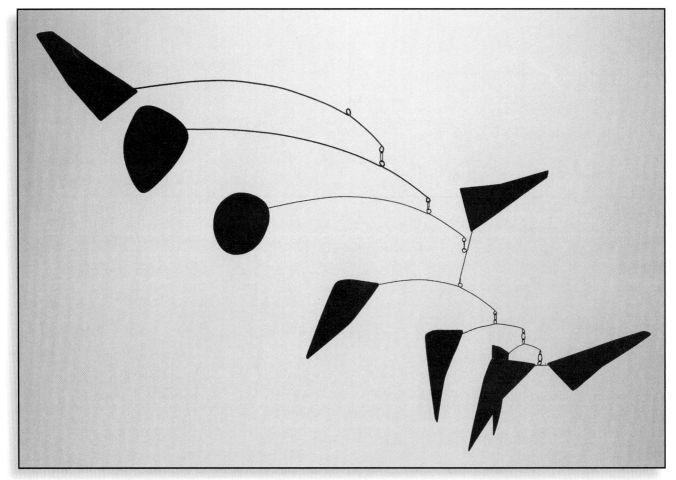

▲ **Alexander Calder.** (American).
Red Rudder in the Air. 1975.
....
Painted sheet metal and steel wire.
31 × 68 inches (78.74 × 172.72 cm.).
Grand Rapids Art Museum, Grand Rapids,
Michigan.

Look at these works of art. The artists combined shapes and forms.

Art History and Culture

Alexander Calder created a new art form. He invented the mobile in the 1930s.

▲ **Frank Stella.** (American).
Loomings 3X. 1986.
....
Ink and oil paint on etched magnesium and aluminum.
$142\frac{1}{8} \times 162\frac{1}{2} \times 44$ inches (361 × 412.75 × 111.76 cm.).
Walker Art Center, Minneapolis, Minnesota.

Study the works of art.

▶ Where do you see shapes?

▶ Where do you see forms?

🔍 Aesthetic Perception

Seeing Like an Artist Look at a form. What does it look like from different sides?

Using Shapes and Forms

Shapes have **height** and **width.**
Forms have height, width, and **depth.**

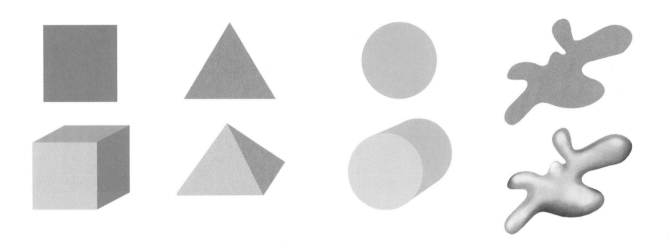

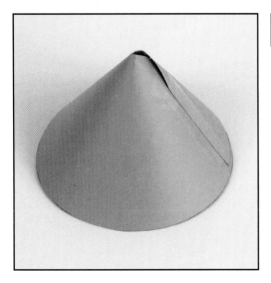

Practice

Make paper shapes into forms.

1. Start with a paper shape.

2. Fold, curl, or bend the paper shape to make a form.

3. Can you measure the depth of your paper form?

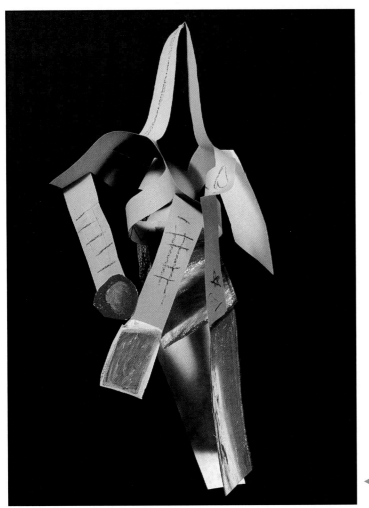

Think about how this student used shapes and forms.

◀ **Carson West.**
Age 5.

Creative Expression

How could you combine shapes and forms to make a mobile?

1. Cut paper into shapes. Twist, fold, or bend some of the shapes into forms.

2. Glue the paper shapes and forms to cardboard.

3. Tie a string to the cardboard.

Art Criticism

Decide Does your mobile look interesting from all sides?

Forms Take up Space

Look at these sculptures. They have forms. They also have open spaces for air to go through.

◀ **George Sugarman.** (American). *Yellow Top.* 1959.

Acrylic on laminated wood. 89 × 46 × 34 inches (226.06 × 116.84 × 86.36 cm.). Walker Art Center, Minneapolis, Minnesota.

Art History and Culture

George Sugarman served in the U.S. Navy. This allowed him to study art through the G.I. Bill program.

Study the works of art.

▶ Where do you see space in and around the sculptures?

◀ **Jacques Lipchitz.** (Lithuanian/American). *Figure.* 1929–1930.

Bronze (cast 137). 7 feet $\frac{1}{4}$ inch × $38\frac{5}{8}$ inches (2.14 meters × 98.11 cm.). Museum of Modern Art, New York, New York.

Aesthetic Perception

Seeing Like an Artist Your hand is a form. Open and close your fingers. How does the space change?

Using Forms and Space

A **form** takes up **space** and has space all around it. A form also can have space inside it or through it.

Practice

Make a human sculpture.

1. Form a group with your classmates.

2. Join hands to make an interesting form.

3. Notice the space around your bodies.

◀ **Alexandra Andrews.**
Age 6.

◀ **Zachary Locotti.**
Age 6.

Think about how these students made designs that take up space.

 **Creative Expression**

What can you design that takes up space?

1. Draw designs on posterboard with crayons and markers.

2. Fold your posterboard in half. Cut slits into it.

3. Bend the posterboard to make some sections stand out.

Art Criticism

Describe Describe your sculpture. What materials did you use to make it?

Free-Form Forms

Look at these sculptures.
They have free-form forms.

◀ **Artist Unknown.** (China).
Standing Youth. Late fifth to early
fourth century B.C.
. . . .
Cast bronze with applied jade. Height 11 13/16 inches
(30 cm.). Museum of Fine Arts, Boston,
Massachusetts.

🏺 Art History and Culture

Standing Youth was made a very long time ago.
It gives clues about the people who lived when it
was made.

Study the sculptures.

▶ What would they look like from each side?

◀ **Barbara Hepworth.** (British).
Figure: Churinga. 1952.
....
Spanish Mahogany. $52\frac{1}{2} \times 16 \times 15\frac{1}{2}$ inches
(133.35 × 40.64 × 39.37 cm.). Walker Art
Center, Minneapolis, Minnesota.

Aesthetic Perception

Design Awareness Which of your toys have geometric forms? Which have free-form forms?

Using Free-Form Forms

Some forms are **geometric forms.**

Other forms are **free-form forms.**

Practice

Sketch a free-form form.

1. Think about what a free-form form looks like from different sides.

2. Sketch the form from different sides.

◀ **Aaron Ragans.**
Age 6.

Think about how this student made
a free-form form.

 **Creative Expression**

How could you create a free-form
sculpture from clay?

1. Think about the forms you
   would see in your sculpture.

2. Mold clay to make free-form
   forms.

3. Join the clay pieces together to
   make your sculpture. Paint the
   sculpture when you are finished.

Art Criticism

Decide Is the clay
sculpture you made a
free-form form?

3-D Me!

Look at the works of art on these pages. They are sculptures of people.

◀ **Artist Unknown.** (Egypt).
Ritual Figure. c. 1962–1928 B.C.
••
Gessoed and painted wood. Height $22\frac{7}{8}$ inches
(58.10 cm.). Metropolitan Museum of Art,
New York, New York.

Art History and Culture

Each of these sculptures represents someone with ideal qualities from the artist's culture.

Study the sculptures.

▶ What forms do you see?

◀ **Artist Unknown.** (China). *Seated Arhat.* c. 1300–1450.

Cast iron, traces of pigment. Height $30\frac{11}{16}$ inches (77.95 cm.). Kimbell Museum of Art, Fort Worth, Texas.

🔍 Aesthetic Perception

Seeing Like an Artist What smaller forms make up your body?

Using People Forms

A person has **height,** **width,** and **depth.**
A person is a form.

Practice

What sizes are the forms of your body?

1. Think about the forms you would show in a sculpture of yourself.

2. Which forms are big? Which forms are small?

3. Sketch the outline of each form.

Think about how this student made a 3-D self-portrait.

◀ **Nicole Nelson.**
Age 7.

Creative Expression

How could you show three dimensions of yourself?

1. Start with a chunk of clay for the torso. Form a neck and head.

2. Make arms and legs and attach them.

3. Add details to make your sculpture look like you.

Art Criticism

Analyze Did you join free-form forms to make your 3-D self-portrait?

Buildings and Spaces

▲ **Artist Unknown.**
(United States). *Corn Palace.* c. 1892.
Mitchell, South Dakota.

Look at the buildings on these pages. The buildings have different forms and open spaces.

Art History and Culture

The *Corn Palace* is decorated with corn and other grains. It was built so farmers could show the richness of the harvest.

▲ **Central Office of Architecture.**
(Los Angeles, California).
The Dwell House. 2003.

Study the buildings.

► What forms do you see?

► What open spaces do you see?

► Are there spaces you cannot see?

Aesthetic Perception

Design Awareness Think about your school building. What forms and spaces does it have?

Using Buildings and Spaces

Buildings are forms. The forms have open spaces for people to move through.

Practice

How are different buildings and spaces used?

1. Think about places to live, learn, shop, play, or work.

2. Describe different buildings and their spaces.

3. How are the places the same? How are they different?

◀ **Nick Byers.**
Age 5.

Think about how this student designed
a building.

Creative Expression

How would you design the home
of an imaginary creature?

1. Use boxes, tubes, bottles, and
   other objects.

2. Join the objects together with
   tape and glue.

3. Paint the house.

Art Criticism

Analyze What shapes
and forms does your
house have?

▲ **Patricia Walker.**
(American). *Still Life.*
1995.
....
Oil on canvas. 22 × 22 inches
(55.88 × 55.88 cm.).
Collection of the artist.

Look at the paintings. The artists showed objects and the space around them.

Art History and Culture

These paintings are still lifes. Artists have been painting still lifes for over 400 years.

◀ **Gabriele Munter.**
(German).
*Still Life with
Porcelain Dog.* 1911.
....
Oil on canvas. $25\frac{3}{4} \times 21\frac{1}{4}$
inches (65.41 × 53.98 cm.).
San Diego Museum of Art,
San Diego, California.

Study the works of art on these pages.

▶ Where do you see space in the pictures?

Aesthetic Perception

Seeing Like an Artist Place two objects on your desk. How can you change the space around them?

Using Space in Pictures

Space is the emptiness around and between objects.

Practice

Look at the space around objects.

1. Look at an arrangement of objects. Look down at it from above.

2. Sketch the space around the objects.

3. Look at the objects from the front. How does the space look now?

▲ **Ali M. Forbes.** Age 7.

Think about how this student showed space around the objects.

 **Creative Expression**

How could you show space around objects?

1. Look at a still-life arrangement.

2. Draw the outlines of the objects. Show the space.

3. Paint your still life.

Art Criticism

Describe What objects are in your still life?

Form and Space

▲ **Artist Unknown.** (Romania, Hamangia Culture). *The Thinker.* 5500–4700 B.C.
Clay. Height 4½ inches (11.43 cm.). National History Museum, Bucharest, Romania.

Art Criticism — Critical Thinking

Describe

▶ What is the person doing?

Analyze

▶ Where do you see empty spaces between parts of the form?

Interpret

▶ How do you think the person is feeling?

Decide

▶ How do you think it would feel to touch something as old as this work?

Show What You Know

Write your answers on a sheet of paper.

1 Choose the form.

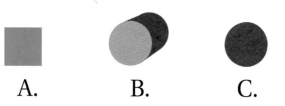

A.   B.   C.

2 Choose the free-form form.

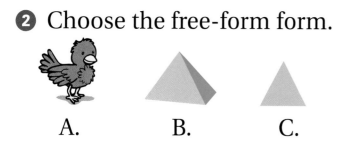

A.   B.   C.

3 Choose the form that has space through it.

A.   B.   C.

Architecture

Think about your neighborhood. What do the buildings look like? Are there parks?

Architects design buildings. They decide how a building will be used and what it will look like.

Landscape architects design places with plants. They think about how the shapes and colors of different plants will look together.

▲ Architect

Form and Space in Theatre

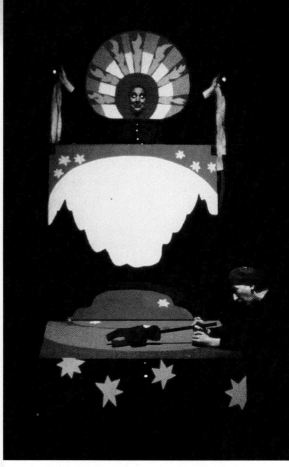

On the Day You Were Born is a play. It tells about events in nature that happened on the day a child was born. The artists and actors explore space and different forms. They use puppets, paintings, poems, and music.

What to Do Use body movements to represent an event in nature.

1. Work with a partner or a group. Choose an event that happens in nature. You could choose rain falling or a tree growing.

2. Make up movements that represent the event. Use your bodies to make forms. Move through space in different ways.

3. Share your movements with others.

▲ In the Heart of the Beast Puppet and Mask Theatre. "On the Day You Were Born."

 Art Criticism

Interpret How did it feel to move through space like your natural event?

Texture, Pattern, and Rhythm

Artists show texture, pattern, and rhythm in their works of art.

Texture is how something feels if you touch it. Repeating a shape makes a pattern. Rhythm is a feeling of movement because something repeats.

◀ **Jesús Moroles.** (American). *Granite Weaving.* 1988.

Georgia gray granite. 98 × 74$\frac{1}{2}$ × 11 inches (248.9 × 189.2 × 27.9 cm.). Smithsonian American Art Museum, Washington, D.C.

Look for **texture, pattern,** and **rhythm** in the sculpture.

▶ What would the work feel like if you could touch it?

▶ What things are repeated?

▶ How do your eyes move around the picture?

In This Unit you will:

▶ learn about texture, pattern, and rhythm.

▶ find texture, pattern, and rhythm in art and the environment.

▶ create art that has texture, pattern, and rhythm.

Jesús Moroles

(1950-   )

▶ is an American artist.

▶ creates large sculptures.

▶ sculpts only granite.

Real Texture

▲ **Artist Unknown.** (United States).
Potawatomi Turban. c. 1880.
Otter pelt, silk ribbon, glass beads. $6\frac{1}{4}$ inches high (15.88 cm.). Chandler-Pohrt Collection, Detroit Institute of the Arts, Detroit, Michigan.

Look at the works of art on these pages. They are real objects.

Art History and Culture

Native Americans made art with materials that came from plants and animals.

Study the objects.

▶ What would they feel like if you touched them?

◀ **Artist Unknown.** (Mi'kmaq People, Nova Scotia, Canada). *Letter Holder or Book Cover.* 1900–1925.

Birch bark decorated with porcupine quills, glass beads, and silk. $14\frac{1}{2} \times 10\frac{1}{4}$ inches (36.83 × 26.04 cm.). Museum of International Folk Art, Santa Fe, New Mexico.

Aesthetic Perception

Design Awareness Touch some objects in the room. Describe their textures.

Using Real Texture

Texture you can feel is called **real texture.**

Practice

Sort things by how they feel.

1. Your teacher will give each student an object.

2. Touch the object you received. What texture does it have?

3. Raise your hand when your teacher calls the name of your object's texture.

▲ **Titi Lola Abisoye.** Age 6.

Think about how this student used real texture in a collage.

 **Creative Expression**

How could you make a **collage** with real texture?

1. Choose materials with different textures.

2. Cut or tear them into geometric and free-form shapes.

3. Arrange the materials. Glue them to the paper.

Art Criticism

Analyze What shapes and textures did you include in your collage?

Visual Texture

Look at the paintings on these pages. The artists showed the textures of the people and objects.

◀ **John Singleton Copley.** (American). *Mrs. Ezekiel Goldthwait.* 1771.

Oil on canvas. $50\frac{3}{8} \times 40\frac{1}{4}$ inches (127.95 × 102.24 cm.). Museum of Fine Arts, Boston, Massachusetts.

Art History and Culture

Before photography was common, artists painted portraits of people.

◀ **Winslow Homer.** (American).
The Lookout—"All's Well". 1896.
....
Oil on canvas. 40 × 30¼ inches (101.6 × 76.84 cm.).
Museum of Fine Arts, Boston, Massachusetts.

Study the paintings to find texture.

▶ What looks smooth?

▶ What looks rough?

🔍 Aesthetic Perception

Seeing Like an Artist Look in a mirror. What textures would you show in a self-portrait?

Using Visual Texture

Texture you can see but not feel is called
visual texture.

Practice

Look for texture in pictures.

1. Look through a magazine.
2. Find pictures that show texture.
3. How many textures can you find in the same picture?

Think about how this student showed texture in her self-portrait.

 Creative Expression

How could you show the textures of you?

1. Draw your self-portrait with crayon.

2. Use lines that show the textures of your body and clothing.

3. Paint over your drawing with watercolors.

Art Criticism

Interpret What mood do you have in your self-portrait? How did you show this?

Raised Texture

◀ **Artist Unknown.**
(Panama). *Plaque.*
700–1100 A.D.
• •
Gold. $9 \times 8\frac{1}{2}$ inches (22.9 ×
21.6 cm.). The Brooklyn Museum,
New York, New York.

Look at the works of art on these
pages. They have raised areas that would
feel bumpy if you could touch them.

Art History and Culture

The *Plaque* looks shiny but it is actually very old! It
is made of gold, which lasts for a very long time.

Study the objects.

▶ Where do you see raised areas?

▲ **Artist Unknown.** (Vizarron, Queretaro, Mexico). *Tortilla Molds.* 1930s.

Carved wood. Approx. 10 × 2 inches (25.4 × 5.08 cm.). San Antonio Museum of Art, San Antonio, Texas.

Aesthetic Perception

Design Awareness What things in your school or home have texture because of raised areas?

Using Raised Texture

Artists create raised areas in their works of art by **carving** and pressing. Works of art with raised areas have real texture.

Practice

Carve and press texture into clay.

1. Experiment with different carving tools.

2. Try pressing something into the clay.

3. Talk about the results.

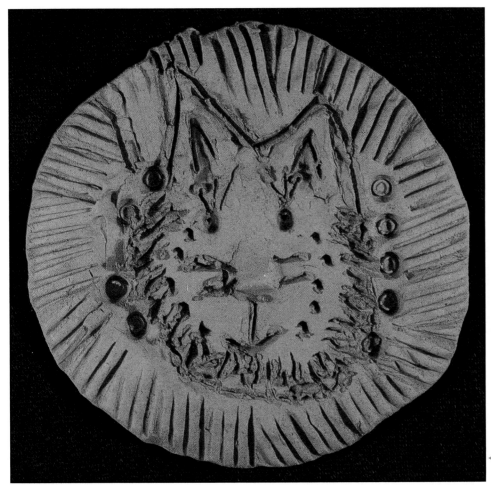

Think about how this student carved real texture.

◀ **Amy Marie Kuhn.**
Age 5.

Creative Expression

How could you carve real texture into clay?

1. Flatten a ball of clay into a square or circle.

2. Carve and press different lines and shapes into the clay to make a design.

3. Carve your initials on the back of the clay.

Art Criticism

Describe What image or design did you carve into your plaque?

Pattern

◀ **Harrison Mc Intosh.** (American).
Stoneware Vase #661. 1966.
∙∙∙
Glazed stoneware. $15\frac{1}{4} \times 13$ inches (38.74 ×
33.02 cm.). Renwick Gallery, Smithsonian American
Art Museum, Washington, D.C.

Look at these works of art. Notice the colors and shapes the artists used to decorate the vase and the quilt.

Art History and Culture

How do you think these works of art could be used in everyday life?

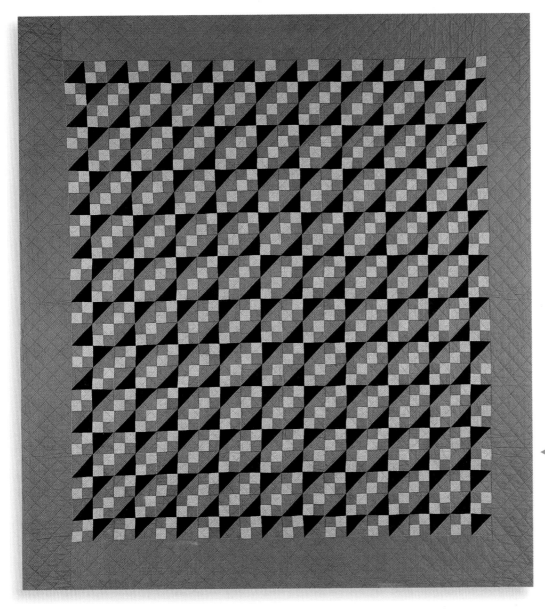

◀ **Barbara Zook Peachey.** (American). *Four Patch in Triangles Quilt.* 1910–1920.

Cotton. $85\frac{1}{2} \times 78\frac{3}{4}$ inches (217.17 × 200 cm.). American Folk Art Museum, New York, New York.

Study the works of art.

▶ What shapes and colors are repeated?

🔍 Aesthetic Perception

Design Awareness Look at your clothing. Find a pattern.

Using Pattern

Repeating a line, a shape, or a color creates
a **pattern.**

Practice

Make a pattern.

1. Use the paper shapes your teacher gives you.
2. Repeat them to make a design that has a pattern.
3. What other patterns could you make?

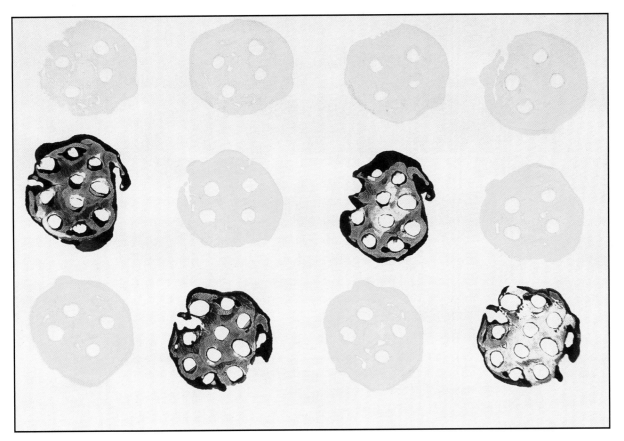

▲ **Brian Schmidt.**
Age 7.

Think about how this student created a pattern.

Creative Expression

What kind of pattern could you use in an artwork?

1. Carve texture into clay to make a stamp.
2. Press the stamp in paint and then on your paper.
3. Make a design that has a pattern.

Art Criticism

Decide Did you repeat a shape to make a pattern?

Changing Pattern

◄ **Artist Unknown.**
(Ashanti Peoples, Ghana).
Kente Cloth.
....
Museum of International Folk Art,
Santa Fe, New Mexico.

Look at the works of art on these
pages. They have patterns.

Art History and Culture

The Ashanti people are well known for their
tradition of weaving kente cloths. There are many
kente patterns. Each one has its own name.

Study the patterns in each work of art.

▶ What lines, shapes, or colors are repeated?

▶ Do they change within each pattern?

◀ **Martha Berry.** (American).
Dance by Numbers
Bandolier Bag. 2000.

Wool, cotton cloth, cotton binding, Czech glass seed beads, yarn, and brass trade beads. 36 × 16 × $\frac{1}{2}$ inches (91.44 × 40.64 × 1.27 cm.). Private Collection.

Aesthetic Perception

Design Awareness What things in your home or school have changing patterns?

Using Changing Patterns

A **motif** is the line, shape, or color that is repeated in a pattern. If you use more than one motif, you have a changing pattern.

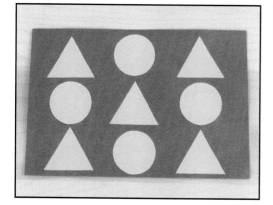

Practice

Use the paper shapes to make patterns.

1. Repeat one motif to make a regular pattern.

2. Say the name of the motif as you point to each shape.

3. Choose two motifs. Make a changing pattern. Say the name of the motif as you point to each one.

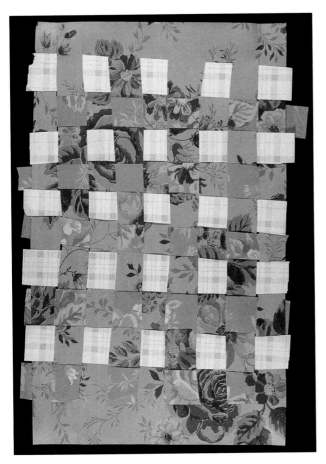

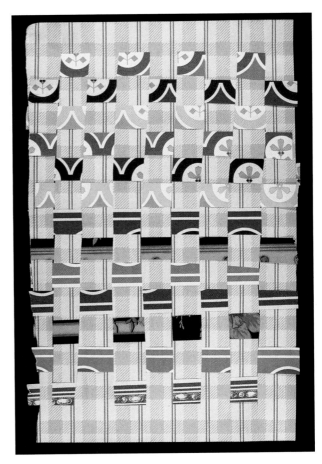

▲ **Brianna Kittle.** Age 6.

▲ **Daniel Tomlinson.** Age 6.

Think about how these students created changing patterns.

Creative Expression

How can you **weave** a pattern?

1. Make a paper loom. Your teacher will show you how.

2. Cut strips of paper.

3. Weave the strips over and under the loom.

Art Criticism

Describe What colors did you use for your weaving?

Lesson 6 Rhythm

▲ **Harry Fonseca.** (American). *Coyote Koshare.* 1993.

Mixed media on canvas. 24 × 30 inches (60.96 × 76.2 cm.). Courtesy of Harry Fonseca.

Look at the works of art on these pages. The artists repeated motifs.

🏺 Art History and Culture

These works of art are *narrative* paintings. Narrative paintings tell a story.

▲ **Antonio Ruiz.** (Mexican).
School Children on Parade.
1936.

Oil on canvas. $9\frac{1}{2} \times 13\frac{1}{4}$ inches (24.13 $\times$ 33.66 cm.). The Metropolitan Museum of Art, New York, New York.

Study the works of art.

▶ What motifs are repeated?

Aesthetic Perception

Seeing Like an Artist Have you seen any repeated motifs in nature?

Using Rhythm

Rhythm is a feeling of movement. Artists create rhythm by repeating motifs. Your eyes move along the artwork. They follow the things that are repeated.

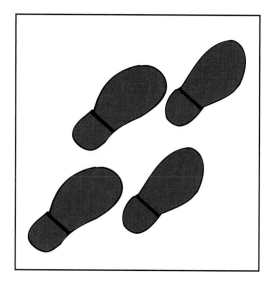

Practice

Create rhythm by walking.

1. Plan a way you could walk in a parade. You could march with a steady beat. Or, you could take a step and then rest.

2. Perform your walk for your classmates. Repeating your steps creates rhythm.

Think about how these students created rhythm.

 Creative Expression

How could you create rhythm in a picture of a parade?

1. Choose a parade theme. Think about what to include. Make yourself an important part of the parade.

2. Draw your parade. Repeat a motif to create rhythm.

Art Criticism

Analyze How do your eyes move through your picture?

Texture, Pattern, and Rhythm

▲ **Artist Unknown.** (Hmong Peoples, Asia).
Hmong Story Cloth. c. 1988.

Cotton. 18 × 18 inches (45.72 × 45.72 cm.).
Private Collection.

Art Criticism — Critical Thinking

Describe

▶ Describe the people you see in this picture.

Analyze

▶ Where do you see rough and smooth textures?

Interpret

▶ What is happening in this picture? Tell the story of these people.

Decide

▶ Does this picture tell an interesting story?

Show What You Know

Write your answers on a sheet of paper.

1 Which of these has smooth texture?

A.   B.   C.

2 Which of these does not have raised texture?

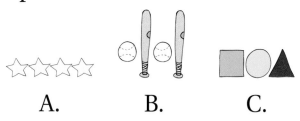

A.   B.   C.

3 Which of these is a changing pattern?

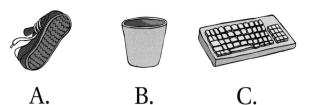

A.   B.   C.

LET'S VISIT A MUSEUM

Kimbell Art Museum

This museum is in Fort Worth, Texas. Many paintings and sculptures are exhibited there. The museum also has art workshops for children.

Texture, Pattern, and Rhythm in Dance

The Nutcracker is a traditional holiday ballet. Colorful, textured dolls and flowers come to life and dance. The music has rhythm.

What to Do Create a mechanical doll dance with a partner.

1. One person is the doll. The other person "winds up" the doll with an imaginary key. Then the person turns on the doll's switch.

2. The doll dances in a mechanical way. The other person turns off the doll's switch. The doll freezes.

3. Switch roles. Perform for the class.

▲ The Joffrey Ballet of Chicago. *The Nutcracker,* "Waltz of the Flowers" excerpt and "The Story of the Nutcracker."

 **Art Criticism**

Analyze What kind of rhythm made the doll seem mechanical?

Balance, Emphasis, and Unity

This artwork is one of the most famous paintings in the world.

It has balance, emphasis, and unity.

◀ **Leonardo da Vinci.**
(Italian). *Mona Lisa.*
1503.

Oil on wood. $30\frac{1}{3} \times 20\frac{6}{7}$ inches
(77 × 53 cm.). Louvre, Paris, France.

A shape has **balance** when both halves match.

► Which part of the artwork has balance?

Artists use **emphasis** to show the most important parts of their artwork.

► What area of *Mona Lisa* attracts your attention first?

An artwork has **unity** when everything looks like it belongs together.

► What colors create unity in the artwork?

In This Unit you will:

► learn about balance, emphasis, and unity.

► find balance, emphasis, and unity in art and the environment.

► create art that has balance, emphasis, and unity.

Self-Portrait

Leonardo da Vinci

(1452–1519)

► was an Italian artist and scientist.

► filled more than 100 notebooks with drawings and ideas.

► drew plans for things we use today, such as helicopters.

▲ **Artist Unknown.** (Kuna Peoples, Panama). *Mola*.

Layered and cut fabric with stitchery. Private Collection.

Look at the shirts on these pages. Draw an imaginary line down the middle of each shirt with your finger. The left side of each shirt matches the right side.

Art History and Culture

The word *mola* means "blouse" in the Kuna language.

Study the shirts to see how they are balanced.

▶ What is the same on both sides of the imaginary line?

▶ What is balanced across the middle?

◀ **Artist Unknown.** (United States). *Arapaho Man's Shirt.* c. 1890.

Buckskin and feathers. 40 × 24½ inches (101.6 × 62.2 cm.). Buffalo Bill Historical Center, Cody, Wyoming.

Aesthetic Perception

Design Awareness What furniture can you think of that has a balanced design?

Using Balance

When you draw an imaginary line down the middle of a shape and both sides match, the shape has **balance.** The imaginary line is the line of balance.

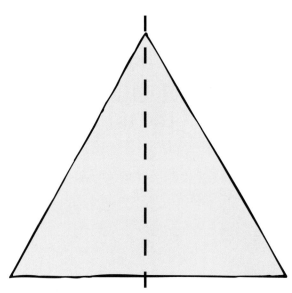

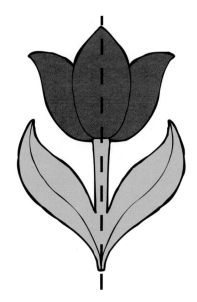

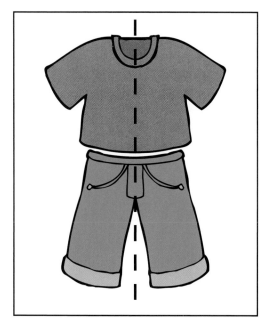

Practice

Look for balance in your classmates' clothing.

1. Look at shirts, pants, jackets, and skirts.
2. Is the shape of the clothing balanced? Is the design on the clothing balanced?
3. Why does clothing usually have balance?

◀ **G. P. Lane.**
Age 7.

Think about how this student designed a balanced shirt.

Creative Expression

How could you design a balanced shirt?

1. Think about symbols you would like to wear on a shirt.

2. Fold your paper in half and open it. Draw half of your shirt design on one half of the paper. Press hard with the oil pastels.

3. Refold your paper. Rub the back. Open the paper.

Art Criticism

Interpret How do the symbols in your shirt design represent you?

Balance in Masks

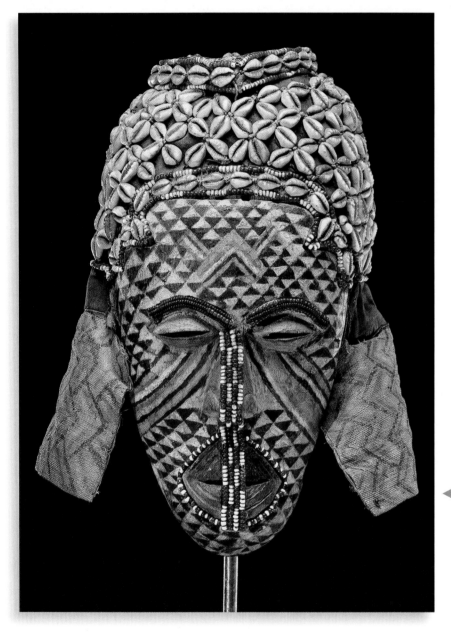

Look at the masks on these pages. Masks are forms that are worn to cover faces.

◀ **Artist Unknown.** (Kuba Peoples, Democratic Republic of the Congo). *Ngady amwaash (Mweel) Mask.* c. 19th–20th century.

Wood, paint, glass beads, cowrie shells, string, raffia, cloth. $12\frac{1}{2} \times 8 \times 9\frac{1}{2}$ inches (31.7 × 20.3 × 24.1 cm.). Virginia Museum of Fine Arts, Richmond, Virginia.

Art History and Culture

These masks represent characters from legends. They were worn for ritual dances.

Study the masks to find balance.

► What is repeated on each half of the masks?

► What is balanced across the middle?

◄ **Joe Seaweed.** (Kwakiutl Peoples, Canada). *Mask of the Moon.* c. 1946.

Cedar bark, mink pelts, plywood. $18\frac{7}{8} \times 4\frac{7}{8}$ inches (47.94 × 12.38 cm.). Seattle Art Museum, Seattle, Washington.

Aesthetic Perception

Seeing Like an Artist What forms found in nature have balance?

Using Balance in Masks

Artists design **masks** with balance because human faces have balance.

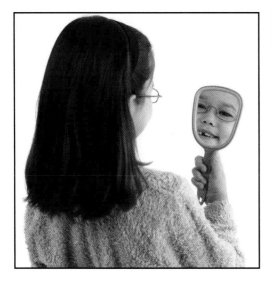

Practice

Look for balance on your face.

1. Look at your face in a mirror.
2. What is repeated on each half?
3. What is balanced across the middle?

Think about how this student created a face with balance.

◀ **Anika Chaturvedi.**
Age 6.

 **Creative Expression**

How could you create a face with balance?

1. Stuff a small paper bag with newspaper to make a head.

2. Use tape to attach a paper towel tube to the head. Cover the tube with fabric to make a body.

3. Attach buttons, yarn, and other objects to the head to make a face with balance.

Art Criticism

Decide Does the face you created have balance?

3 Emphasis in Paintings

Look at the works of art on these pages. The artists included something unusual in the paintings.

◀ **Rene Magritte.** (Belgian).
Time Transfixed. 1938.
Oil on canvas. $27\frac{1}{2} \times 38\frac{1}{2}$ inches (69.85 × 97.79 cm.).
The Art Institute of Chicago, Chicago, Illinois.

Art History and Culture

These artists were famous for painting pictures that look like dreams. This style was popular at the time.

Study the works of art.

▶ What stands out in each painting?

▲ **Marc Chagall.** (Russian).
Birthday. 1945.

Oil on cardboard. $31\frac{3}{4} \times 39\frac{1}{4}$ inches (80.65 $\times$ 99.67 cm.). Museum of Modern Art, New York, New York.

Seeing Like an Artist Look around your classroom. Has your teacher made anything stand out?

Using Emphasis in Paintings

When an object stands out, it has **emphasis.** Artists create emphasis by making an object look different from what the viewer might expect.

How can you arrange crayons to create emphasis?

1. Look through your crayon box. Find four colors that are similar.

2. Find one crayon that is different. Arrange the crayons.

3. Ask a classmate, "Which crayon do you notice first?"

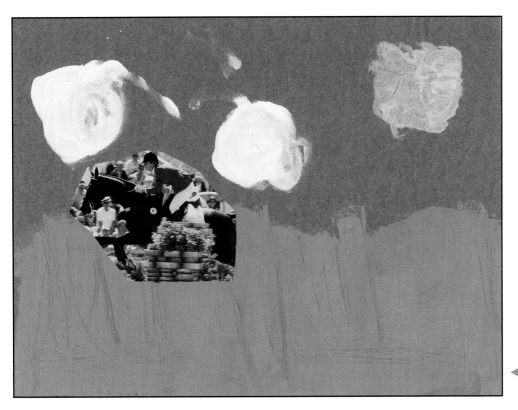

Think about how this student created emphasis in the landscape.

Creative Expression

How could you create a landscape with emphasis?

1. Look through a magazine. Find a picture of an object you would find outside.

2. Carefully cut out the object.

3. Glue the object to a sheet of paper. Draw and paint a landscape around the object.

Art Criticism

Analyze How did you create emphasis in your landscape?

Emphasis in Forms

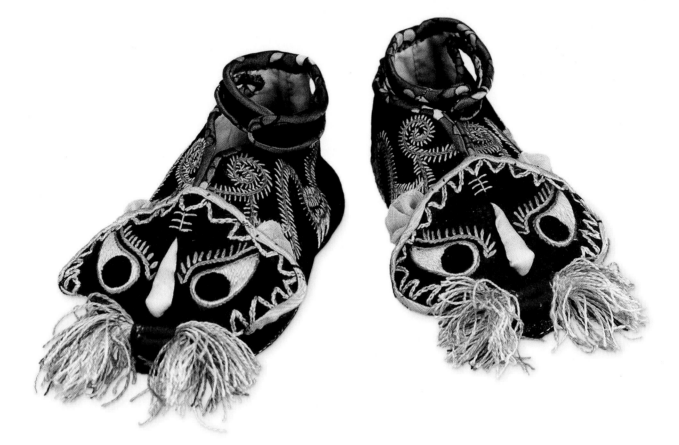

▲ **Artist Unknown.** (China). *Chinese Children's Slippers.* 1991.

Cotton appliquéd with silk. 4 × 2 × 1½ inches.
(10.16 × 5.08 × 3.81 cm.). Private collection.

Look at the shoes on these pages.
The artists decorated them.

Art History and Culture

The tiger faces on the front of the slippers in
Chinese Children's Slippers were put there to watch
over a child's steps as the child learned to walk.

▲ **Artist Unknown.**
(United States). *Sioux Moccasins.* c. 1900.
Cowhides, rawhide, porcupine quills, glass beads, metallic beads, cotton fabric, tin cones, and dyed horsehair. $10\frac{3}{4}$ inches (27.3 cm.). Detroit Institute of Arts, Detroit, Michigan.

Study the shoes. Imagine that someone is wearing them.

▶ If you saw that person walking, what part of the shoes would you notice first?

Aesthetic Perception

Design Awareness Have you ever seen a police car? What part of it did you notice first?

Using Emphasis in Forms

Artists can decorate forms to make one part stand out. Artists create **emphasis** by using textures, colors, or shapes that are different from other areas.

Practice

Which part of your shoe is emphasized?

1. Look at your shoes.
2. What part do you like best? Why?
3. How is that part of your shoe different?

◄ **Christopher Dickhute.**
Age 7.
Tyler Ferguson.
Age 7.
Chase Rantamaki.
Age 6.
Adam Sanders.
Age 6.

Think about how these students created emphasis on the slippers.

 **Creative Expression**

How could you emphasize the front of a slipper?

1. Trace your foot on a sheet of construction paper. Cut out the foot shape.

2. Glue a strip of paper to make the top of the slipper.

3. Decorate the top of the slipper. Make it look like an animal.

Art Criticism

Describe What shapes and colors are on your slipper?

Unity with Words and Symbols

▲ **Stuart Davis.**
(American). *Visa.* 1951.
Oil on canvas. 40 × 52 inches
(101.6 × 132.08 cm.). Museum of
Modern Art, New York, New York.

Look at the works of art on these pages. The artists used pictures and words or symbols to make a design.

Art History and Culture

Ida Kohlmeyer used pictographs, or symbols that represent words, in her artwork. How many pictographs do you recognize?

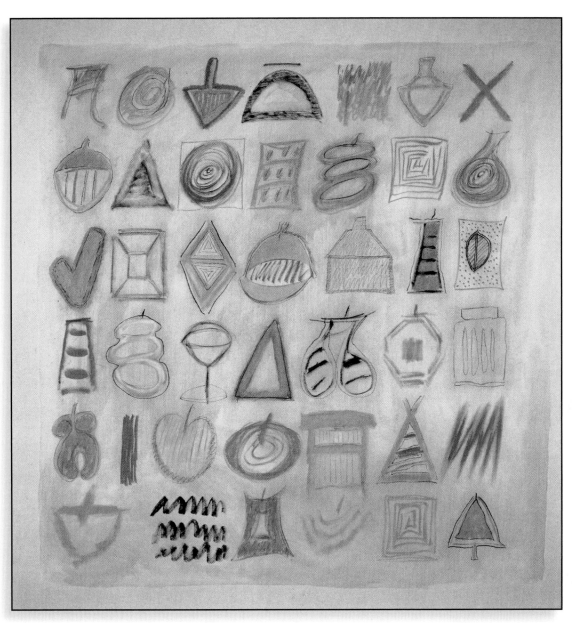

▲ **Ida Kohlmeyer.**
(American).
Symbols. 1981.
....
Oil, graphite, and pastel on
canvas. $69\frac{1}{2} \times 69$ inches
(176.53 × 175.26 cm.).
National Museum of
Women in the Arts,
Washington, D.C.

Study the works of art.

▶ What lines, shapes, or colors make each artwork look like everything belongs together?

Aesthetic Perception

Seeing Like an Artist What are some places you see words and art together?

Using Unity with Words

A work of art has **unity** when everything looks like it belongs together. Lines, shapes, and colors can connect pictures with words or symbols to create unity.

Practice

Find words or symbols combined with pictures in magazines.

1. Look through magazines.

2. Find pages where words or symbols are combined with pictures.

3. How do the pages have unity?

Think about how this student combined pictures with a symbol.

◀ **Joseph Lazzari.**
Age 6.

Creative Expression

How could you make an imaginary creature from a letter of the alphabet?

1. Think of your favorite letter. You could choose one of your initials.

2. Draw the letter. Imagine how the shape of the letter could become an animal, person, or creature.

3. Add more lines and shapes to complete the creature.

Art Criticism

Analyze How do the lines, shapes, and colors create unity in your picture?

Unity in Sculpture

◀ **Gilda Snowden.** (American). *Monument.* 1988.
. . . .
Encaustic on wood. 76 × 81 × 8 inches (193 × 205.7 × 20.3 cm.). Detroit Institute of Arts, Detroit, Michigan.

Look at the works of art on these pages. Each artist put smaller forms together to make a sculpture.

 Art History and Culture

Gilda Snowden created *Monument* as a tribute to her parents. The artwork has symbols that remind her of her family.

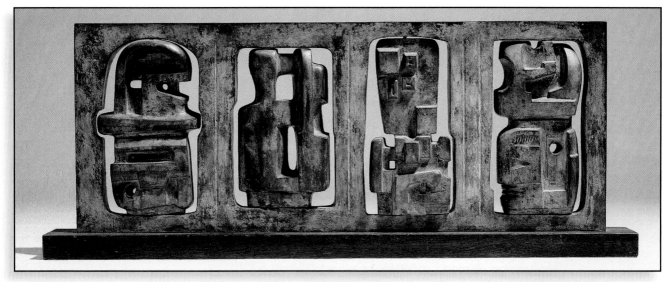

▲ **Henry Moore.** (British). *Study for Time-Life Frieze.* 1952.
....
Bronze. $14\frac{7}{8} \times 38\frac{3}{4} \times 1\frac{11}{16}$ inches (37.78 × 98.43 × 4.29 cm.). Walker Art Center, Minneapolis, Minnesota.

Study the sculptures.

▶ What forms are alike in each sculpture?

▶ What colors did the artists repeat?

Aesthetic Perception

Design Awareness What forms are repeated throughout your classroom?

Using Unity in Sculpture

Colors and forms that are alike create **unity** in **sculpture.**

Think of pieces of furniture that have unity.

1. List pieces of furniture in your home.

2. Think about colors and forms that are repeated in each piece of furniture.

3. Why does furniture have unity?

Think about how this student created unity in the sculpture.

Creative Expression

How can you create a sculpture with unity?

1. Select wood scraps to use in your sculpture.

2. Arrange the wood scraps on a board. Glue them together.

3. Paint your sculpture.

Art Criticism

Describe What colors and forms did you use in your sculpture?

Balance, Emphasis, and Unity

▲ **Miriam Schapiro.** (Canadian/American).
Offering. 2002.
Acrylic and fabric on canvas. 60 × 58 inches (152.4 × 147.32 cm.).
Private collection.

Art Criticism | Critical Thinking

Describe

▶ What do you see in this painting?

Analyze

▶ What part of this painting has balance?

Interpret

▶ What is the mood of this painting?

Decide

▶ Do you think this painting has a story to share with others?

Balance, Emphasis, and Unity, continued

Show What You Know

Write your answers on a sheet of paper.

1 Which of these shapes has balance?

A.　　　B.　　　C.

2 Which of these does not show emphasis?

A.　　　B.　　　C.

3 Colors and forms that are alike can create _____ in sculpture.

A. emphasis

B. movement

C. unity

Balance, Emphasis, and Unity in Stories

Let Them Eat Books is a show for children. The actors perform stories from all over the world.

What to Do Build a story with a group.

1. Sit in a circle. One person holds the story stick.

2. The person with the story stick starts the story. After two sentences, that person passes the story stick to the next person.

3. Go around the circle. The last person has to end the story.

▲ We Tell Stories. "Let Them Eat Books."

 **Art Criticism**

Describe Describe the beginning, middle, and end of the story.

Technique Tips

Drawing

Pencil

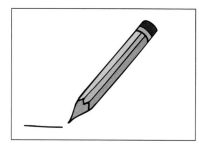

Thin lines

Thick lines

Crayon

Thin lines

Thick lines

Large spaces

Small dots

Large dots

Technique Tips

Crayon Rubbing

Rub away from your holding hand.

Marker

Use the tip.

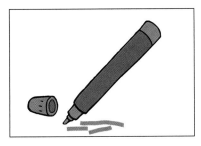

Use the side of the tip.

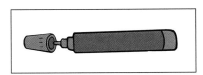

Put on the cap.

Technique Tips

Oil Pastel

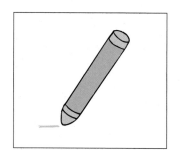

Lines

Color in large spaces.

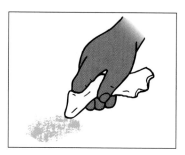

Blend colors.

Colored Chalk

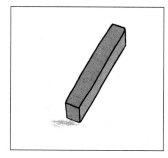

Lines

Color in large spaces.

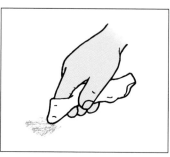

Blend colors.

Painting

Taking Care of Your Paintbrush

Rinse and blot to change colors.

Technique Tips

Taking Care of Your Paintbrush

Clean your brush when you are done.

1. Rinse.

2. Wash with soap.

3. Rinse again.

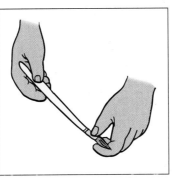

4. Shape.

5. Store.

Technique Tips

Tempera

Wipe the brush.

Mix the paint on a palette.

Use a wide brush for large spaces.

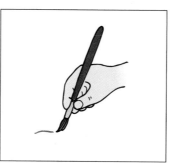

Use a thin, pointed brush for details.

Technique Tips

Watercolor

Put water on each color.

Dip the brush in the paint.

Mix on a palette.

Press firmly for thick lines.

Press lightly for thin lines.

Watercolor Resist

Crayons and oil pastels show through.

Technique Tips

Painting Rough Texture with Watercolor

1. Dip the brush in water.

2. Hold the brush over a container. Squeeze water out.

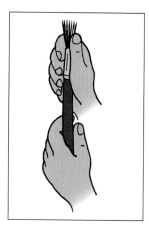

3. Divide the bristles into spikes.

4. Dip the brush in paint. Lightly touch the brush to paper.

5. Rinse. Shape the bristles into a point.

Technique Tips

Collage

Using Scissors

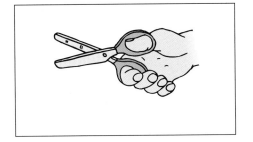

Hold scissors this way.

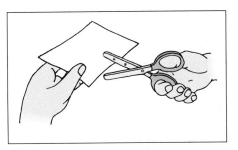

Hold the paper by its edge with your other hand.

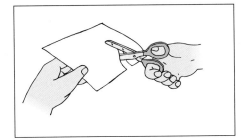

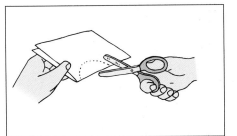

Always cut away from your body.

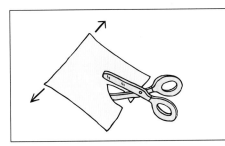

Have a friend stretch cloth as you cut.

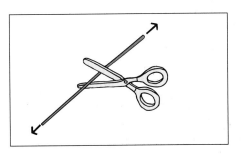

Do the same with yarn.

Technique Tips

Using Glue

Use only a few glue dots on one paper.

Smooth with the tip of the glue bottle.

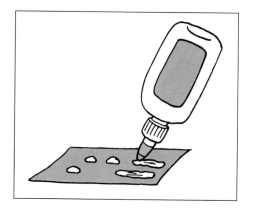

Press the papers together.

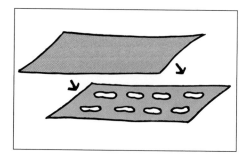

Close the bottle and clean the top.

Technique Tips

Arranging a Design

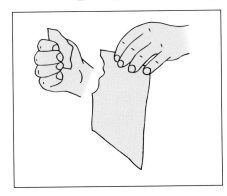

Tear shapes.

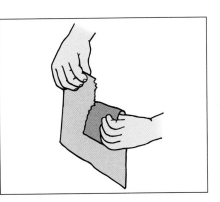

Tear strips.

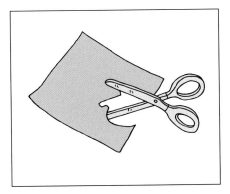

Cut shapes.

Use found objects.

Make a design.

Glue the pieces
into place.

Technique Tips

Paper Sculpture

Making Strip Forms

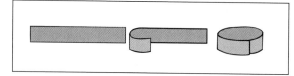

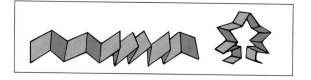

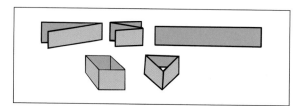

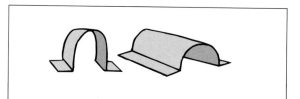

Use paper strips to make stairs, stars, tunnels, and other things.

Cones

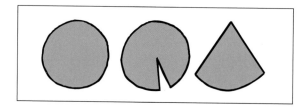

Building with Forms

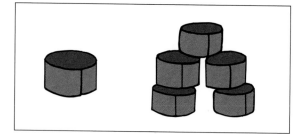

Technique Tips

Weaving

Making a Paper Loom

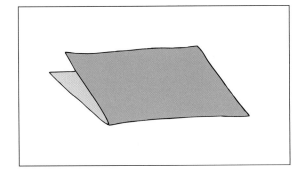

1. Fold paper in half.

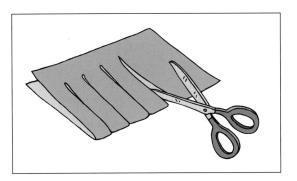

2. Cut wide strips from the folded edge. Don't cut to the other edge.

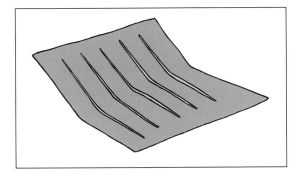

3. Open the paper.

Weaving on a Paper Loom

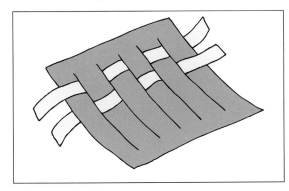

Over and under.

Technique Tips

Printmaking

Making a Stamp Print

1. Paint the stamp.

Or, press the stamp into a paint-filled sponge.

2. Press the stamp onto paper and lift.

Using a Brayer

1. Roll the brayer through the ink.

2. Roll the brayer over a leaf.

3. Press the leaf onto paper and lift.

Technique Tips

Printmaking

Making a Sponge Print

Use a different sponge for each color. Dip a sponge in paint. Press it onto paper.

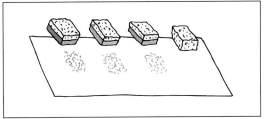

Making a Stencil

Cut a shape from folded paper.

Sponge Printing with a Stencil

Hold the stencil in place. Press paint into the stencil with a sponge.

Technique Tips

Printmaking

Monoprint

1. Make a design in paint.

2. Lay paper on top. Rub the back.

3. Peel away the paper.

Technique Tips

Transfer Print

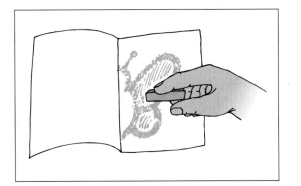

1. Fold paper in half. Unfold and draw on one half.

2. Refold the paper and rub.

3. Open the paper.

Technique Tips

Sculpting
Working with Clay

Squeeze, pull, and shape the clay to make it soft. Form clay into an oval shape.

Squeeze and pinch.

Pinch and pull.

....

Adding Texture to Clay

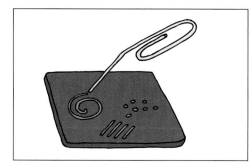

Carve the clay. Use a pointed tool.

Press an object that has texture into the clay.

Technique Tips

Sculpting
Joining Clay

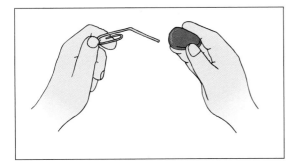

Score the edge.

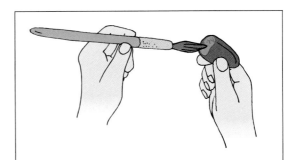

Apply slip.

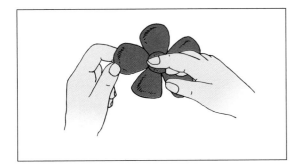

Squeeze and smooth.

Stitchery
The Running Stitch

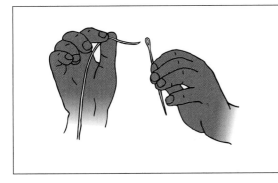

Thread a needle.

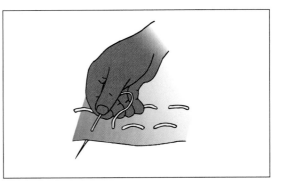

Use a running stitch.

Activity Tips

Lines

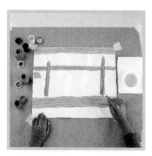

🎨 **Creative Expression**

1. Think of a design you can make with thick, thin, smooth, rough, solid, and broken lines.

2. Fill your paper with lines.

3. Brush watercolor paint over your lines.

Calm Lines

🎨 **Creative Expression**

1. Start your landscape with calm lines.

2. You can add other lines to complete your picture.

3. Fill the page.

Activity Tips

Diagonal Lines

🎨 **Creative Expression**

1. Think about how a tree changes as it grows.

2. Tear a sheet of paper to make a tree trunk. Tear thick branches and thin branches. Tear leaves.

3. Glue your tree onto another sheet of paper.

Curved Lines

🎨 **Creative Expression**

1. Tape a square of plastic wrap to the table. Spread paint on it.

2. Pull a comb through the paint to make curved lines. Use gentle movement.

3. Lay paper on top of the paint to make a print.

Activity Tips

Unit 1 · Lesson 5 **Buildings Have Lines**

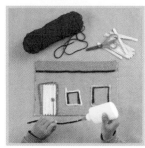

🎨 **Creative Expression**

1. Start with a piece of cardboard for the building.

2. Use different objects to add parts to the building. Add windows, doors, and a roof.

3. What else can you add to make the building unique?

Unit 1 · Lesson 6 **Lines Show Movement**

🎨 **Creative Expression**

1. Think about the lines that show this movement.

2. Use the brush tool in your computer's paint program to draw yourself at play.

3. Fill the page.

Activity Tips

Lines Outline Shapes

🎨 **Creative Expression**

1. Use crayons to draw outlines of fish shapes and plant shapes.

2. Use big shapes, medium-sized shapes, and small shapes.

3. Brush watercolor over your page.

Geometric Shapes

🎨 **Creative Expression**

1. Make texture rubbings on paper.

2. Trace the outlines of geometric shapes on the paper.

3. Cut out the shapes. Arrange them to make a design. Glue the shapes to black paper.

Activity Tips

Free-Form Shapes

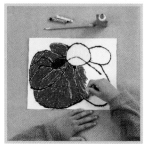

🎨 Creative Expression

1. Sketch a free-form shape you found in a magazine.

2. Go over the lines with black glue.

3. When the glue is dry, color your picture with pastels.

Unit 2 · Lesson 4 **People Shapes**

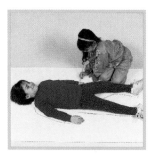

🎨 Creative Expression

1. Lie on a large piece of paper.

2. Have a partner trace the outline of your body.

3. Paint your portrait with tempera paints.

Activity Tips

Unit 2 · Lesson 5 — Shapes of People in Action

🎨 Creative Expression

1. Think about what your body looks like when you play your favorite game.

2. Draw yourself at play. Use action shapes to show how you move.

Unit 2 · Lesson 6 — Still-Life Shapes

🎨 Creative Expression

1. Choose your objects. Decide how you would arrange them.

2. Use the shape tools in your computer's paint program to draw objects with geometric shapes. Use the brush tool to draw objects with free-form shapes.

3. Use the fill tool to paint the objects. Use other tools to decorate your picture.

Activity Tips

A Rainbow of Colors

🎨 **Creative Expression**

1. Think of objects you would like to make colorful. Draw the outlines of the objects with a black marker.

2. Using crayons, color the objects with rainbow colors in order.

3. Paint the background with rainbow colors in order.

Primary Colors

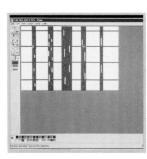

🎨 **Creative Expression**

1. Use the computer's paint program. Choose a primary color to draw horizontal and vertical lines that represent streets.

2. Use the other primary colors to draw lines that represent cars and trucks on the streets.

3. Draw primary-colored shapes to represent buildings in the white space.

Activity Tips

Unit 3 · Lesson 3 **Red and Yellow Make Orange**

🎨 **Creative Expression**

1. Think of a shape for yellow and one for red. Paint your shapes.

2. Mix red and yellow paint to make orange. See how many oranges you can make.

3. Fill the rest of the paper with orange.

Unit 3 · Lesson 4 **Blue and Yellow Make Green**

🎨 **Creative Expression**

1. Imagine a summer day outdoors. Choose green things to put in your scene.

2. Make green things by mixing blue and yellow.

3. Use blue and yellow to fill the background.

Activity Tips

Unit 3 · Lesson 5 **Red and Blue Make Violet**

🎨 **Creative Expression**

1. Overlap torn pieces of red and blue tissue paper.

2. Glue the tissue paper to a sheet of white paper to make the shape of your creature.

3. Add details to your creature with black marker.

Unit 3 · Lesson 6 **Primary and Secondary Colors**

🎨 **Creative Expression**

1. Fold your paper in half. On one half, paint squares of each primary color. On the other half, paint squares of the primary color needed to make each secondary color.

2. Fold your paper and press to mix the paint.

3. Use craft sticks to draw your scene in the wet paint.

Activity Tips

Shapes and Forms

🎨 Creative Expression

1. Cut paper into shapes. Twist, fold, or bend some of the shapes into forms.

2. Glue the paper shapes and forms to cardboard.

3. Tie a string to the cardboard.

Forms Take Up Space

🎨 Creative Expression

1. Draw designs on posterboard with crayons and markers.

2. Fold your posterboard in half. Cut slits into it.

3. Bend the posterboard to make some sections stand out.

Activity Tips

Free-Form Forms

 **Creative Expression**

1. Think about the forms you would see in your sculpture.

2. Mold clay to make free-form forms.

3. Join the clay pieces together to make your sculpture. Paint the sculpture when you are finished.

3-D Me!

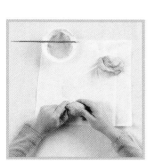

Creative Expression

1. Start with a chunk of clay for the torso. Form a neck and head.

2. Make arms and legs and attach them.

3. Add details to make your sculpture look like you.

Activity Tips

Buildings and Spaces

🎨 **Creative Expression**

1. Use boxes, tubes, bottles, and other objects.
2. Join the objects together with tape and glue.
3. Paint the house.

Space in Pictures

🎨 **Creative Expression**

1. Look at a still-life arrangement.
2. Draw the outlines of the objects. Show the space.
3. Paint your still life.

Activity Tips

Real Texture

🎨 **Creative Expression**

1. Choose materials with different textures.

2. Cut or tear them into geometric and free-form shapes.

3. Arrange the materials. Glue them to the paper.

- -

Visual Texture

🎨 **Creative Expression**

1. Draw your self-portrait with crayon.

2. Use lines that show the textures of your body and clothing.

3. Paint over your drawing with watercolors.

Activity Tips

Raised Texture

🎨 Creative Expression

1. Flatten a ball of clay into a square or circle.

2. Carve and press different lines and shapes into the clay to make a design.

3. Carve your initials into the back of the clay.

Pattern

🎨 Creative Expression

1. Carve texture into clay to make a stamp.

2. Press the stamp in paint and then on your paper.

3. Make a design that has a pattern.

Activity Tips

Unit 5 · Lesson 5 **Changing Pattern**

🎨 **Creative Expression**

1. Make a paper loom. Your teacher will show you how.

2. Cut strips of paper.

3. Weave the strips over and under the loom.

Unit 5 · Lesson 6 **Rhythm**

🎨 **Creative Expression**

1. Choose a parade theme. Think about what to include. Make yourself an important part of the parade.

2. Draw your parade. Repeat a motif to create rhythm.

Activity Tips

Balance

🎨 **Creative Expression**

1. Think about the symbols you would like to wear on a shirt.

2. Fold your paper in half and open it. Draw half of your shirt design on one half of the paper. Press hard with the oil pastels.

3. Refold your paper. Rub the back. Open the paper.

Balance in Masks

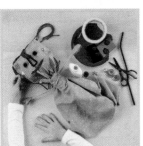

🎨 **Creative Expression**

1. Stuff a small paper bag with newspaper to make a head.

2. Use tape to attach a paper-towel tube to the head. Cover the tube with fabric to make a body.

3. Attach buttons, yarn, and other objects to the head to make a face with balance.

Activity Tips

Emphasis in Paintings

 Creative Expression

1. Look through a magazine. Find a picture of an object you would normally find outside.

2. Carefully cut out the object.

3. Glue the object to a sheet of paper. Draw and paint a landscape around the object.

- -

Emphasis in Forms

 Creative Expression

1. Trace your foot on a sheet of construction paper. Cut out the foot shape.

2. Glue a strip of paper to make the top of the slipper.

3. Decorate the top of the slipper. Make it look like an animal.

Activity Tips

Unity with Words and Symbols

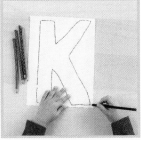

Creative Expression

1. Think of your favorite letter. You could choose one of your initials.
2. Draw the letter. Imagine how the shape of the letter could become an animal, person, or creature.
3. Add more lines and shapes to complete the picture.

Unity in Sculpture

Creative Expression

1. Select wood scraps to use in your sculpture.
2. Arrange the wood scraps on a board. Glue them together.
3. Paint your sculpture.

Visual Index

Artist Unknown
The Thinker
5500–4700 B.C.
(page 150)

Artist Unknown
Standing Youth
late 5th–early 4th
century B.C. (page 134)

Artist Unknown
Ritual Figure
c. 1962–1928 B.C.
(page 138)

Artist Unknown
Plaque
A.D. 700–1100. (page 164)

Artist Unknown
Seated Arhat
c. 1300–1450. (page 139)

Leonardo da Vinci
Mona Lisa
1503. (page 184)

Albrecht Dürer
Rhinoceros
1515. (page 34)

John Singleton Copley
Mrs. Ezekiel Goldthwait
1771. (page 160)

Artist Unknown
*Ngady Amwaash
(Mweel) Mask*
c. 19th–20th century.
(page 190)

Artist Unknown
Bridal Bed Cover
19th century.
(page 49)

Artist Unknown
Potawatomi Turban
c. 1880. (page 156)

Artist Unknown
Arapaho Man's Shirt
c. 1890. (page 187)

Artist Unknown
Corn Palace
c. 1892. (page 142)

Winslow Homer
The Lookout—"All's Well"
1896. (page 161)

Artist Unknown
Man's Headband of
Toucan Feathers
c. 20th century.
(page 104)

Artist Unknown
Kente Cloth
20th century. (page 172)

Artist Unknown
Mola
20th century.
(page 186)

Artist Unknown
Sioux Moccasins
c. 1900. (page 199)

Artist Unknown
Letter Holder or Book Cover
c. 1900–1925. (page 157)

Henri Matisse
A Glimpse of Notre Dame in the Late Afternoon
1902. (page 113)

Mary Cassatt
In the Garden
1904. (page 94)

Paul Cézanne
Still Life with Apples and Peaches
c. 1905. (page 86)

Albert Marquet
Le Pont Saint-Michel in Paris
1908. (page 71)

Henri Rousseau
The Equatorial Jungle
1909. (page 74)

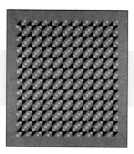

Barbara Zook Peachey
Four Patch in Triangles Quilt
1910–1920. (page 169)

Gabriele Münter
Still Life with Porcelain Dog
1911. (page 147)

Maurice Prendergast
Summer, New England
1912. (page 117)

Piet Mondrian
Composition V
1914. (page 41)

Seldon Conner Gile
Two Fishermen and a Boat
c. 1917. (page 101)

Lawren S. Harris
Shacks
1919. (page 52)

Joaquín Torres-García
New York City
Bird's Eye View
c. 1920. (page 36)

Wassily Kandinsky
Composition 8
1923. (page 37)

Pablo Picasso
The Red Foulard
1924. (page 87)

Jacques Lipchitz
Figure
1929–30.
(page 131)

Artist Unknown
Tortilla Molds
1930s. (page 165)

Pierre Bonnard
The Breakfast Room
1930–1931.
(page 90)

Agnes Tait
Skating in Central Park
1934. (page 48)

Blanche Lazzell
*The Monongahela
at Morgantown*
1935. (page 53)

Antonio Ruiz
School Children on Parade
1936. (page 177)

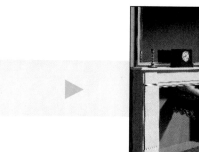

René Magritte
Time Transfixed
1938. (page 194)

Georgia O'Keeffe
Papaw Tree– 'Iao Valley
1939. (page 109)

Isabel Bishop
Ice Cream Cones
1942. (page 79)

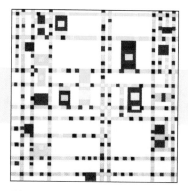

Piet Mondrian
Broadway Boogie Woogie
1942–1943. (page 100)

Thomas Hart Benton
July Hay
1943. (page 116)

Marc Chagall
Birthday
1945. (page 195)

Joe Seaweed
Mask of the Moon
c. 1946. (page 191)

Harrison Begay
Night Chant Ceremonial Hunt
1947. (page 57)

Jacob Lawrence
Children at Play
1947. (page 56)

Auguste Herbin
Vie no. 1 (Life No. 1)
1950. (page 70)

Stuart Davis
Visa
1951. (page 202)

Barbara Hepworth
Figure: Churinga
1952. (page 135)

Henry Moore
Study for Time-Life Frieze
1952. (page 207)

Hans Hofmann
Au Printemps, Springtime
1955. (page 120)

Rufino Tamayo
Toast to the Sun
1956. (page 105)

George Sugarman
Yellow Top
1959. (page 130)

Grace Hartigan
Dido
1960. (page 112)

Harrison Mc Intosh
Stoneware Vase #661
1966. (page 168)

Claes Oldenburg
*Shoestring Potatoes
Spilling from a Bag*
1966. (page 124)

Ellsworth Kelly
Spectrum III
1967. (page 96)

Loïs Mailou Jones
*Esquisse for Ode to
Kinshasa*
1972. (page 64)

Ivan Eyre
Touchwood Hills
1972–1973. (page 108)

Alexander Calder
Red Rudder in the Air
1975. (page 126)

Jacob Lawrence
Builders—Red and Green Ball
1979. (page 82)

Jasper Johns
Between the Clock and the Bed
1981. (page 44)

Ida Kohlmeyer
Symbols
1981. (page 203)

David Hockney
Hollywood Hills House
1982. (page 97)

Frank Stella
Loomings 3X
1986. (page 127)

Artist Unknown
Hmong Story Cloth
c. 1988. (page 180)

Carmen Lomas Garza
Naranjas (Oranges)
1988. (page 78)

Jesús Moroles
Granite Weaving
1988. (page 154)

Gilda Snowden
Monument
1988. (page 206)

Artist Unknown
Chinese Children's Slippers
1991. (page 198)

Deborah Butterfield
Rex
1991. (page 67)

Sylvia Plimack Mangold
The Elm Tree (Summer)
1991. (page 45)

Harry Fonseca
Coyote Koshare
1993. (page 176)

Joseph Norman
Spanish Garden #IV
1994–1995. (page 60)

Janet Fish
Jump
1995. (page 83)

Patricia Walker
Still Life
1995. (page 146)

Francesca Puruntatameri
Muniti Red Snapper
c. 1998. (page 66)

Wolf Kahn
Lilac-colored Landscape
1998. (page 40)

Martha Berry
Dance By Numbers Bandolier Bag
2000. (page 173)

Hung Liu
Hong Shancha: Red Camellia
2002. (page 75)

Miriam Schapiro
Offering
2002. (page 210)

Central Office of Architecture
The Dwell House
2003. (page 143)

Glossary

balance

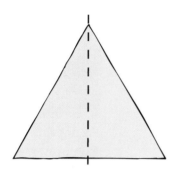

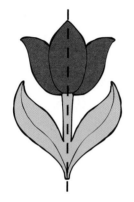

broken line

building
a structure where we live, work, meet, or play

carving

circle

collage
objects glued onto paper

color wheel

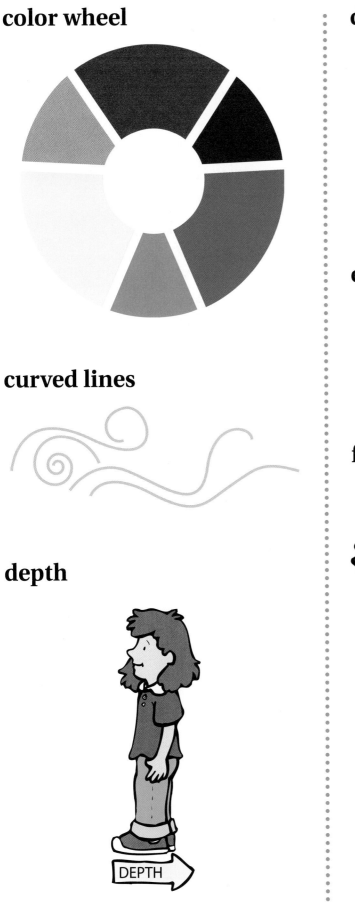

curved lines

depth

diagonal lines

emphasis

forms

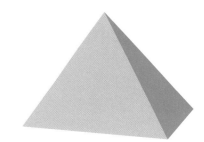

free-form form

free-form shape

geometric form

geometric shapes

height

horizontal lines

landscape

a picture of the outdoors

line

mask

three-dimensional art worn to cover the face

motif

what is repeated in a pattern

outline

pattern

position

how body parts are arranged

primary colors

rainbow

real texture

texture you can feel

rectangle

rhythm

rough line

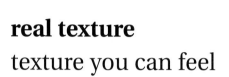

sculpture

art that can be seen from all sides

secondary colors

shapes

smooth line

solid line

space
the emptiness between, around, and within objects

square

still life

texture
the way something feels when you touch it

thick line

thin line

triangle

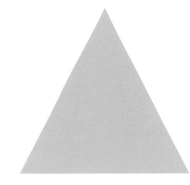

unity

a feeling of belonging together

vertical lines

visual texture

texture you can see but cannot touch

weave

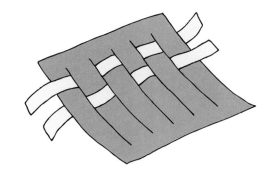

width

WIDTH

zigzag line

Index

Photo Credits

12 (tl)Columbus Museum of Art, Ohio: Museum Purchase, Howard Fund II. ©The Georgia O'Keeffe Foundation/Arts Rights Society (ARS), New York, (bl)The Metropolitan Museum of Art, Gift of Henry G. Marquand, 1897. (97.22.25) Photograph ©2000 The Metropolitan Museum of Art, (br) ©Corbis; 13 (tl)Honolulu Academy of Arts, Honolulu, Hawaii. Gift of James A. Michener, 1976 (16,794), (tr)Smithsonian American Art Museum, Washington, DC. Gift of Catherine McIntosh / Art Resource, NY, (br)Buffalo Bill Historical Center, Cody WY Chandler-Pohrt Collection, Gift of The Searle Family Trust and The Paul Stock Foundation; 14 ©2004 Board of Trustees, National Gallery of Art, Washington, DC. Gift of Edgar William and Bernice Chrysler Garbisch; 15 Georgia Museum of Art - University of Georgia - Athens - Georgia. Eva Underhill Holbrook Memorial Collection of American Art. Gift of Alfred H. Holbrook. ©Jacob and Gwendolyn Lawrence Foundation; 16 The Sidney and Harriet Janis Collection (606.1967) Digital Image ©The Museum of Modern Art/Licensed by SCALA/Art Resource, NY. ©2004 Artist Rights Society (ARS), New York/ADAGP, Paris; 17 The Metropolitan Museum of Art, H.O. Havemeyer Collection, Bequest of Mrs. H.O. Havemeyer, 1929. Photography ©1996 The Metropolitan Museum of Art; 18 ©Carmen Lomas Garza. Photo by Wolfgang Dietze; 21 (t)International Folk Art Foundation Collection. Museum of International Folk Art. Santa Fe, New Mexico. Photo by: Pat Pollard, (b)The Roland P. Murdock Collection, Wichita Art Museum, Wichita, Kansas; 24, 26, 28 Museum of Fine Arts, Houston, Texas. The John A. and Audrey Jones Beck Collection; 34 The Metropolitan Museum of Art, Gift of Junius S. Morgan, 1919. (19.73.159) All rights Reserved, The Metropolitan Museum of Art; 35 SCALA/Art Resource, NY; 36 Yale University Art Gallery - New Haven - Connecticut. Gift of Collection Societe Anonyme. ©2004 Artists Rights Society (ARS), New York/ADAGP, Paris; 37 Photograph by David Heald ©The Solomon R. Guggenheim Foundation, New York. ©2004 Artists Rights Society (ARS), New York/ADAGP, Paris; 40 Courtesy of Thomas Segal Gallery. Jeff Goldman, photographer. ©Wolf Kahn/Licensed by VASA, New York, NY; 41 Digital Image ©The Museum of Modern Art/Licensed by SCALA/Art Resource, NY. ©2004 Artists Rights Society (ARS), New York/ADAGP, Paris; 44 ©Digital Image ©The Museum of Modern Art/Licensed by SCALA/Art Resource, NY. ©Jasper Johns/Licensed by VAGA, New York, NY; 45 Courtesy: Alexander and Bonin, New York, New York; 47 Randy Ellett; 49 International Folk Art Foundation Collection. Museum of International Folk Art. Santa Fe, New Mexico. Photo by: Pat Pollard; 51 Randy Ellett; 53 Amon Carter Museum, Fort Worth, Texas. 1985.287; 55 Randy Ellett; 56 Georgia Museum of Art - University of Georgia - Athens - Georgia. Eva Underhill Holbrook Memorial Collection of American Art. Gift of Alfred H. Holbrook. ©Jacob and Gwendolyn Lawrence Foundation; 57 Museum purchase. The Philbrook Museum of Art, Tulsa, Oklahoma; 59 Randy Ellett; 62 Courtesy of Lawrence C. Zoller; 64 National Museum of Women in the Arts. Gift of Wallace and Wilhelmina Holladay; 65 ©Mohamed Mekkawi/Howard University; 66 ©Tony Haruch; 67 Collection of the Lowe Art Museum, University of Miami. Gift of an Anonymous Donor; 69 Randy Ellett; 70 Collection Albright-Knox Art Gallery, Buffalo, New York. Gift of the Seymour H. Knox Foundation, Inc., 1966; 71 ©SuperStock; 72 Photodisc/Getty Images, Inc; 73 Randy Ellett; 74 National Gallery of Art, Washington D.C. Chester Dale Collection; 76 Taxi/Getty Images, Inc; 77 Randy Ellett; 78 ©Carmen Lomas Garza. Photo by Wolfgang Dietze; 80 ©Eclipse Studios; 82 Francine Seders Gallery LTD, Seattle. Photo by Chris Eden. ©Jacob and Gwendolyn Lawrence Foundation; 83 ©Janet Fish/Licensed By VAGA, New York, NY; 85 Randy Ellett; 86 National Gallery of Art, Washington, D.C. Gift of Eugene and Agnes E. Meyer; 87 Norton Museum of Art, West Palm Beach, Florida, Gift of R.H. Norton, 49.2. ©2004 Estate of Pablo Picasso/Artist Rights Society (ARS), New York; 90 ©Digital Image ©The Museum of Modern Art/Licensed by SCALA/Art Resource, NY. ©2004 Artists Rights Society (ARS), New York/ADAGP, Paris; 92 LWA-Dann Tardif/Corbis; 93 Giannetti Studio; 94 Gift of Dr, Ernest G. Stillman. Photograph © 1995 The Detroit Institute of Arts; 97 Gift of Penny and Mike Winton, 1983. Walker Art Center, Minneapolis, Minnesota; 99 Randy Ellett; 100 ©2004 Artists Rights Society (ARS), New York/ADAGP, Paris; 101 Norton Museum of Art, West Palm Beach, Florida, Purchase, the R.H. Norton Trust, 91.24; 102 ©Eclipse Studios; 105 The Roland P. Murdock Collection, Wichita Art Museum, Wichita, Kansas; 106 ©Eclipse Studios; 107 Randy Ellett; 108 ©National Gallery of Canada, Ottawa. Purchased, 1974; 109 Honolulu Academy of Art, Honolulu, Hawaii. Gift of The Georgia O'Keeffe Foundation, 1994. ©The Georgia O'Keeffe Foundation/Arts Rights Society (ARS) , New York; 110 ©Eclipse Studios; 112 Collection of the McNay Art Museum, Gift of Jane and Arthur Stieren; 113 Collection Albright-Knox Gallery, Buffalo, New York, Gift of Seymour H. Knox, Sr. 1927. ©2004 Succession H. Matisse, Paris/Artist Rights Society (ARS) , New York; 114 ©Eclipse Studios; 115 Randy Ellett; 116 The Metropolitan Museum of Art, George A. Hern Fund, 1943. Photograph ©1982 The Metropolitan Museum of Art. ©T.H. Benton and R.P. Benton Testamentary Trusts/Licensed by VAGA, New York, NY; 117 ©Smithsonian American Art Museum, Washington, DC/Art Resource, NY; 120 From the collection of the late Kathering Sanford Deutsch, class of 1940. Frances Lehman Loeb Art Center, Vassar College, Poughkeepsie, NY; 122 Michal Daniel; 124 Collection Walker Art Center, Minneapolis. Gift of the T.B. Walker Foundation, 1966; 126 ©Grand Rapids Art Museum, Gift of Mr. and Mrs. Miner S. Keeler, 1976.4.1. ©2004 Artists Rights Society (ARS), New York/ADAGP, Paris; 127 ©2004 Artists Rights Society (ARS), New York; 128 ©Eclipse Studios; 129 Randy Ellett; 130 Gift of the T.B. Walker Foundation, 1966; 131 Digital Image ©The Museum of Modern Art/Licensed by SCALA/Art Resource, NY; 133 Randy Ellett; 135 Gift of the T.B. Walker Foundation, 1955; 136 (t) Corbis, (c) ©Photodisc/Getty Images Inc; 137 Randy Ellett; 141 Randy Ellett; 142 Peter Pearson/Stone/Getty Images, Inc; 144 Photodisc/Getty Images, Inc; 147 San Diego Museum of Art, Bequest of Earle W. Grant. ©2004 Artists Rights Society (ARS), New York; 150 ©Natural History Museum, Bucharest, Romania/ Art Resource, NY; 153 Lee Hanson; 154 Smithsonian American Art Museum, Washington, DC/Art Resource, NY; 155 ©Philippe Caron/Corbis Sygma; 156 Cranbrook Institute of Science. Photo ©1992 The Detroit Institute of Arts; 157 International Folk Art Foundation Collection. Museum of International Folk Art. Santa Fe, New Mexico. Photo by: Pat Pollard; 158 (tl, tr) Photodisc/Getty Images, Inc, (b) ©Eclipse Studios; 159 Randy Ellett; 162 Photodisc/Getty Images, Inc; 167 Randy Ellett; 168 Smithsonian American Art Museum, Washington, DC. Gift of Catherine McIntosh/Art Resource, NY; 169 Collection American Folk Art. New York, New York. Gift of Mr. and Mrs. William B. Wigton 1984.25.12. Photo by Schecter Lee; 170 ©Eclipse Studios; 173 Cherokee beadwork artist, Martha Berry. Photograph by Dave Berry; 174,175, 179 Randy Ellett; 182 ©Photography by Louis I. Kahn, Courtesy of the Kimbell Art Museum, Fort Worth, Texas; 183 Herbert Migdoll; 184 Photo ©Erich Lessing/Art Resource, NY; 187 Buffalo Bill Historical Center, Cody WY Chandler-Pohrt Collection, Gift of The Searle Family Trust and The Paul Stock Foundation; 189 Randy Ellett; 190 Virginia Museum of Fine Arts, Richmond. The Arthur and Margaret Glasgow Fund. Katherine Wetzel, photographer; 191 Seattle Art Museum, Gift of John H. Hauberg. Photo by Paul Macapia; 192 ©Eclipse Studios; 193 Randy Ellett; 194 Joseph Winterbotham Collection, 1970.426. Photograph ©200, The Art Institute of Chicago, All Rights Reserved; 195 ©Digital Image ©The Museum of Modern Art/Licensed by SCALA/Art Resource, NY. ©2004 Artists Rights Society (ARS), New York/ADAGP, Paris; 196 ©Eclipse Studios; 199 Founders Society Purchase with fund from Flint Ink Corporation. Photo ©1988 The Detroit Institute of Arts; 200 Taxi/Getty Images, Inc; 201 Randy Ellett; 202 ©Estate of Stuart Davis/Licensed by VAGA, New York, NY; 203 National Museum of Women in the Arts. Gift of Wallace and Wilhelmina Holladay; 205 Randy Ellett; 206 Photograph ©1996 Detroit Institute of Arts, Detroit Art Founders Society Purchase, Chaim, Fanny, Louis, Benjamin, Anne, and Florence Kaufman Memorial Trust; 207 Walker Art Center. Gift of the T.B. Walker Foundation, 1957; 208 Eclipse Studios; 209 Randy Ellett; 210 Courtesy Miriam Schapiro; 212 ©Getty Images Inc; 213 Craig Schwartz; 232 (t) ©Aaron Haupt, (b) ©Eclipse Studios; 233 ©Eclipse Studios; 234 (t) ©Eclipse Studios, (b) ©Matt Meadows; 235 ©Eclipse Studios; 236 (t) ©Aaron Haupt, (b) ©Eclipse Studios; 237(t) ©Matt Meadows, (b) ©Eclipse Studios; 238 (t) ©Eclipse Studios, (b) ©Matt Meadows; 239, 240 ©Eclipse Studios; 241 ©Aaron Haupt; 242 (t) ©Aaron Haupt, (b) ©Eclipse Studios; 243 (t) ©Aaron Haupt, (b) ©Eclipse Studios; 244, 245 ©Aaron Haupt; 246 (t) ©Aaron Haupt, (b) ©Eclipse Studios; 247-249 ©Eclipse Studios.